365 Crochet Patterns Book for 365 Days Of The Year

D1727148

By Coral James

365 Crochet Patterns Book for 365 Days Of The Year

Table of Contents

Coaster; Crochet small heart; Floral heart motif; Arch Bracelet; Martis Bracelets; Crochet Beaded Bracelet; Tunisian Check Scrubbie; Honey Earrings; Flower Applique; Pendant Necklace; Bead Stripped Poach; Adria Earrings; Chic Pincushion; Pearly Heart Charm; Bumps and Ridges Washcloth; Sparkly Beaded Crochet Bracelet; Beaded Bangles

March: Tatted Earring; Small Tatted Earring; Tatted Earring Pattern; Cute Girly Earring; Crochet Earring; Tatted Earring; Jewel Earring; Tatted Earring; Decorative Letter I; Spring Flowers Bookmark; Floral Bookmark Tatting Pattern; Beginners 2 Strand Crochet Afghan Pattern; Summer Coaster; Crochet Button Earrings; Flamingo Seat Cover; Bath Mat; Classic Bath Mat; Beautiful Bath Mat; Curtain Bracelet; Wreath curtain pull; Curtain tie back pattern; Crocheted Towel Topper; Lazy Wave Hand Towel; Hand Warmers; Dish Towel; One Skein Tunisian Scarf; Royal Splendor Afghan; Afghan Stitch Coaster; Bridal hankie; Bridal Garter; Cotton Wreath Tube Chain

April: Roanoke Dishcloth; The Dandelion Dishcloth; Beginners 2 Strand Crochet Afghan Pattern; Basketweave Crochet Afghan Pattern; Diamond Duo Scarf; DC Keyhole Neck Scarf; Diamond Stitch Neck Scarf; Draft dodger scarf; Earthen Lace scarf; Easy and Warm 2 Stitch Scarf; Simple Crochet Scarf; Flower Scarf; Frosty Scarf; Gina' s Crochet Basket weave; Crochet Dish Cloth; Easy Baby Blanket;

Baby Washcloth; Back Scrubber; Mossy washcloth; Spa cloth; Scrubby Washcloth; Towel Ring; Placemat Set; Sunrise Placemat; Sunrise Coaster; Pineapple Runner; Coral Reef Motif; Mid-sized Placemat; Kentucky Placemat; Aqua Toilet Seat Cover

May: 100 Yard Dash; Scarf; Easy Soft Scarf; Shell Scarf; Fake afghan stitch scarf; Adult Scarf; Neck Cozy; 2 strand chunky cowl scarf; Rippling Peacock Scarf; Faux fabric Circle scarf; Arch Mesh scarf; Ashlea scarf; Basic Crocheted Neck Warmer; Cozy Crocheted Scarf; Five Petal Crocheted Flower; Crossed in the middle Scarf; Family Hat; Bling Bling and Little flowers; Flirty Kristen; Bubbles; Bumpy Scarf pattern; Arithmancy scarf; Brite Scarf; Brite Hat; Chained Fringe Scarf; Chakra scarf; Chevron Scarf; Claudia Scarf; Caitlin' s V-Stitch Scarf; Tablecloth Motif; Square Pillow pattern

June: Father' s Day Fold and Sew Wallet; Spiral Coaster; Gift Card Holder; Business Card Holder; Business Card Sleeve; Extra Large Coaster; Fingerless Gloves; Soda Can Cozy; Coffee Cup Sleeve; Amazing Pillow Pattern; Oriental Pillow Pattern; Frills Pillow Pattern; Elizabethan rose tablecloth motif; Studio Couch Pillow pattern; Bath Mat Pattern; Fathers' Day Classic Cotton Belt; Beautiful Leaves; Belt Design; Tartsy Bookmarks; Holly Bookmark; Facecloth; Big Bob Washcloth; Hand Towel; Alora Earrings; Coffeemaker Cozy; Open Cuff Bracelet; Upside Down Earrings; Fresh Floral Face Cloth; Dish Soap Apron; Doll Basket .

July: Textured Washcloth; Cleaning Pads; Nano Cozy; Crochet Rib Mug Cozy; Granny Stripe Cup Cozy; Mug Tie Cozy; Kindle Sleeve; Warm Hat; Ear Warmer; Fusion Throw; iPod Cozy; Scarf Striped; Keyhole Scarf; Triple Warm Ear Warmer; Slide-In iPod Nano Sleeve; Wannabe Scarf; Easy Dish Cloth; Filet Dad Bookmark; Bug Scrubbie; Mesh Soap Saver; Tatting A 3-Color Flower; Medium Motif; Large Motif; Alice Insertion; Blue Doily; Blue Motif Pattern; Sampler Square; Tilted Square; Window Square; Bunny Finger Puppet; Mug Cozy

August: Autumn Harvest Scarf; Block Tunisian Scarf for Barbie; Cable Bow; Tripoint Bookmark; Beanie for Barbie Doll; Seashore Dishcloth; Talia Earrings; Pop Out Flower; Peek-a-Boo Mug Cozy; iPod Cozy; Thick Pot Handle Cozy; Chapstick Keychain Cozy; Slouchy Beanie; Open Tunisian Scarf; Spring Choker; Badge Holder; Cat Scrubbie; Cat Ear Headband; Cat Toy; Miss Mouse Cat Trip Toy; No-Sew Pencil Skirt; Lemon Cake Cozy; Craft Bangles; French Press Cozy Pattern; Water Bottle Cozy; Soap Holder; Leaf Cozy; Brown Cozy; Detachable Monkey Ears; Cotton Sleeve; Hemp Sleeve

September: Comfortable Mug Cozy; Monster Apple Crochet Cozy; French Mug Cozy; iPod Crochet Pattern; Mayflower Necklace; Tiara Headband; Summer Waves Crochet Placemat Pattern; Summer Waves Crochet Coaster Pattern; Crochet Placemat; Lace Flower; Puffy Flower Coaster; Shell Bracelet; Easy Pen Case; Sparkly Crescent; Classic Square Coaster; Tunisian Heart Coaster; Square Coaster; Spoked Coaster; Stem Glass Scarf; Crayon Link Scarf; Mimosa Scarf; Knot Stitch Shawl; Keychain Card Holder; Lip Balm Holder; Watermelon Potholder; Octopus Holder; Water Bottle Holder; Classic Lanyard; Ear Warmer; Wrist Cuff

October: Itty Bitty Hat; Expanding Pentagon Motif; Lucky Star Motif; Mini Motif; Concave Motif; Open Star Motif; Skull Motif; Doll Cape; Rose Earrings; Blue & White Earrings; Ankle Bracelet; Wrist Warmers; Pocket Purse; Eye Glass Caddie; Envelope; Twist Headband; Rustic Star Ornament; Beaded Circle Pendant; Mini Wreath; Squircle Earrings; Simple Twist Cuff; Mug Cozy; Snowflake Mug Cozy; Spiral Flower Pattern; Beaded Eyewear; Chair Cushion; Easy Glasses Case; Homespun Scarf; Chunky Chain Scarf; Open Tunisian Scarf; Knot Bracelet

November: Cellphone Cozy; Fuzzy Neck Warmer; Apple Cozy; Scarf Pattern; Abstract Autumn Scarf; Scarflet; Ridged Scarf; Lemonade Scarf Pattern;

Infinity Scarf; Lightning Scarf; Lime Green Cowl; Tab Cowl; Beautiful Angel Barbie Head; Baby Powder Cover; Coaster Crochet Pattern; Penny Coaster; 29 Stitch Dishcloth; Magic dishcloth pattern; Slouchy Hat; Curtain Tie Back; Badge Holder; Pen Holder; Fancy Cowl; Easy Neck Warmer; Offset Back scrubber; Open Ridge Washcloth; Bath Milt Single Crochet; Comfortable bath loofah; Bathroom Rug; Easy Bath Puff

December: Mini Santa Hat; Barbie Doll Santa Claus Hat; Bobble Bowl; Winter Chill Christmas Ornament; Christmas Pickle; Christmas Tree Ornament Stuffed; Christmas Wreath Applique; 3 Holly Berries; 3 Holly Leaves; Christmas Ball Ornaments; Daisy Coaster; Sunny Day Coaster; Ruffled Coaster; Wheel Coaster; Openwork Tie; Berny Stitch Tie; Crochet Men's Bowtie; Shell Stitch Tie; Men's infinity scarf pattern; Ripple Tie; Simple Tie Gift; Animator's Hat; The Husband Hat; Man's Hat; Crocheted Wedding Bow Tie; Bev's Grown-Ups Easy 'Booties'; Fingerless Gloves for Men; Basketball Hoop; Little Boys' Bobble Scarf; Alpaca Weave Scarf; Lizzy Scarf Pattern

Conclusion.

Introduction

Hello Crochet Lovers,

In this book we will have different, neat and amazing crochet patterns that you can use every single day of the year. We will share crochet patterns in here that you can try out from time to time. There are more crochet patterns out there than we can begin to fathom, so to make things easier we will come up with categories that can help you keep track of what you are doing.

One of the best things that you will come to realize so far is that you can never run out of ideas when it comes to crocheting patterns. There are endless patterns that you can work around, and these will come in handy for your crochet projects.

To make it easier for you to follow these steps to the letter, there are images that show you what the final design looks like!

This book is an incredible crotchet guide, so that whenever you are feeling stuck, you can easily refer to it and make some progress with the crocheting work.

Have a happy experience crocheting!

Abbreviations

Throughout this book, the following are the abbreviations that we will be using:

+	Join
-	Picot
Beg	Begin/Beginning
BLO	Back Loop Only
CC	Contrasting Color
CH	Chain
CM	Centimeter
CL	Cluster
FPDC	Front Post Double Crochet
DC	Double Crochet
DC3TOG	Double Crochet 3 together
DEC	Decrease
DPN	Double Pointed Needles
DTR	Double Treble Crochet
FLO	Front Loop Only
FSC	Foundation Single Crochet

HDC	Half double crochet
INC	Increase
J	Join
LP/LPS	Loop/Loops
MC	Main Color
P	Small joining picot
R	Ring
REP	Repeat
REV	Reverse
RND/RNDS	Round/Rounds
RS	Right Side
RW	Reverse Work
SC	Single Crochet
SDSP	Seed Spike Stitch
SK	Skip
SL ST	Slip Stitch
Sm R	Small Ring
SP/SPS	Space/ Spaces
SR	Split Ring
ST/STS	Stitch/ Stitches
TBS	Tunisian Bar Stitch

TDC	Triple Double Crochet
TKS	Tunisian Knit Stitch
TOG	Together
TR	Treble Crochet
TSS	Tunisian Simple Stitch
WS	Wrong Side
YO	Yarn Over
YOH	Yarn Over Hook

January

January 1 Scrubbing Dishcloth

Materials:

Red Heart - 4ply WW Yarn

Hook Size G (for yarn)

Hook Size P (for netting)

Instructions

R1: With netting, using P Hook, ch4, 11dc in 4th ch from hook. Join with sl st in top of beg ch4.

Fasten off and weave ends. -RS-

R2: With RS facing using the G hook, join yarn with sl st in any dc.

Ch3, 2dc in same st. Work 3dc in ea rem dc. (36dc)

Join with sl st in top of beg ch3.

R3: Ch3, do not turn. (dc, ch2, dc) in next dc (center dc of 3dc group).

Dc in next dc. *Dc in next dc. (dc, ch2, dc) in next dc. Dc in next dc.

Rep from * around. Join with sl st in top of beg ch3.

R4: Ch3. Dc in ea dc. (2dc, ch2, 2dc) in ea ch2 sp around. Join with sl st in top of beg ch3.

R5: Rep R4.

Fasten Off.

January 2 Dahlia Dishcloth

Materials

Lily Sugar'n Cream (70.9 g/2.5 oz; 109 m/120 yds)

Contrast A (01215 Robin's Egg) 1 ball

Contrast B (00042 Tea Rose) 1 ball

Contrast C (00073 Sunshine) 1 ball

Size 5 mm (U.S. H or 8) crochet hook or size needed to obtain gauge.

Instructions

With A, ch 8. Join with sl st to form ring.

1st rnd: Ch 1. Work 16 sc in ring. Join B with sl st to first sc.

2nd rnd: With B, ch 4 (counts as tr). 1 tr in same sp as sl st. 2 tr in each sc around. Join with sl st to top of ch 4. 32 sts.

3rd rnd: Ch 4 (counts as tr). (Yoh) twice and draw up a loop in same sp as last sl st. (Yoh and draw through 2 loops on hook) twice. *(Yoh) twice and draw up a loop in next tr. (Yoh and draw through 2 loops on hook) twice. Rep from * once more. Yoh and draw through all 4 loops on hook – counts as cluster. **Ch 3. (Yoh) twice and draw up a loop in same sp as last tr. (Yoh and draw through 2 loops on hook) twice. [(Yoh) twice and draw up a loop in next tr. (Yoh and draw through 2 loops on hook) twice] twice. Yoh and draw through all 4 loops on hook –cluster made. Rep from ** to end of rnd. Ch 3. Join C with sl st to top of first cluster.

4th rnd: With C, ch 6. Sl st in 4th ch from hook. 3 tr in same sp as sl st at end of 3rd rnd. 1 sc in top of next cluster. *Ch 6. Sl st in 4th ch from hook. 3 tr in same sp as last sc. 1 sc in top of next cluster. Rep from * around.

Join with sl st to base of first cluster. Fasten off.

January 3 Sun Catcher Dishcloth

Materials

Acrylic yarn

size I hooks

Instructions

In magic circle, work 7 sc. Join with slip stich to top of 1st sc.

2. ch1, work 2 sc in same sp & each sc around. join. (14 sc)

3. ch3 (counts as 1 hdc and 1 ch st for this round), hdc in same sp, [ch 1, sk1 sc, (hdc,ch1,hdc) in next sc]6x, ch 1, join.(14 ch-1 sps & 14 hdc)

4. ch1, 2sc in same sp, sc in next st, *2sc in next stitch, 1 sc in next 2 stitches, repeat from * around. Join. (36 sc)

5. ch4 (counts as 1 dc & 1 ch-1 sp), dc in same sp, * sk 1 sc, (dc, ch1, dc) in next sc, repeat from * around. Join to 3rd chain of beg. ch-4. (18 ch-1 sps)

6. ch1, sc in same sp, sc in ch-1 sp, *2sc in next stitch, sc in next 4 sts, repeat from * around, ending w 2 sc in 2nd to last stitch of row. Join to 1st sc. (64 sc)

7. ch1, sc in same sp, (ch3, sk 1 sc, sc in next sc) around. Join to 1st sc. (32 ch-3 sps)

8. sl st 1X to land in ch-3 sp, ch4, dc in same sp, * (dc, ch2, dc) in next ch-3 sp, repeat from * around.(32 ch-2 sps)

9. ch 1, *sc in next ch-2 sp, ch3, sc in same sp, repeat from * around. Finish off, and weave in ends.

January 4 Angel Dishcloth

Materials:

1 ball 100% cotton yarn

2" plastic ring

Size G crochet hook.

Instructions:

1). 40 sc inside the ring, join with sl st to beginning stitch, ch 3, turn.

2). Dc in same st as joining, 2 dc in next 11 sc, ch 3, turn.

3). Dc in same st as joining, 2 dc in each dc across, ch 3, turn.

4). Dc in same as joining, dc in next dc, 2 dc in next dc, repeat across, ch 3, turn.

5). Dc in same st as joining, dc in each dc across, ch 3, turn.

6). Repeat row 5. Fasten off.

7). Join in 21st dc across, ch 3, dc in each of the next 34 dc, ch 3, turn.

8). 2 dc in each dc across, ch 3, turn.

9-11). Dc in each dc across, ch 3, turn. At the end of row 11, fasten off.

12). Join at beginning of either wing, ch 1, sc around whole entire dishcloth, excluding the head, making sure you fasten wings down beforehand, so that only the outer edge of wings is included in the sc's.

January 5 Twisted Melon Dishcloth

Materials

Cotton yarn

4.5 mm hook.

Instructions

Row 1:

Ch 30. Sc in 3rd ch from hook. * Dc in next st, sc in next st.* Repeat from * to * Across. Dc in last st. Ch 2. Turn.

Rows 2-15:

Sk first dc. *Dc in bl of next sc (from previous row), Sc in bl of next dc (from previous row).* Repeat from * to * across. Dc in Ch 2 of previous row. Ch 2. Turn.

Row 16:

Sk first dc. *Dc in bl of next sc (from previous row), Sc in bl of next dc (from previous row).* Repeat from * to * across. Dc in Ch 2 of previous row.

Round 17:

Ch 1. Turn. Evenly sc around, placing 2 sc's in ea corner. Ss to join. Fasten Off.

January 6 Mesh Dishcloth

Materials

A ball of cotton yarn, a hook F size

Instructions

Chain 31, loosely.

Dc in 3rd ch from hook, *skip 1 ch, ch1, dc in next ch*, rep to end of row, ending ch 2, turn.

Dc in ch sp, ch 1, repeat to end, ending dc around turning ch, ch2, turn.

Repeat this row until you have a square shape (approx 15 rows).

You could add some sort of edging if you like.

Adjust the size as you see fit, chaining a multiple of 2 plus 1.

Set the colours by soaking the item in a water and vinegar mixture for a while, though this doesn't always help.

January 7 Afghan Stitch Dishcloth

Materials:

Hook: Size J Afghan Hook

Yarn: Sugar and Cream 4 ply 100% Cotton Fashion Yarn (Less than 2.5 oz)

Instructions

Step 1: Make a base chain with the required number of stitches. Insert hook in 2nd ch from hk and draw through a lp. Leave this lp on the hook. Pull a lp through each ch, leaving them on the hk, to the end of the row.

Step 2: Work the return row from left to right. Do not turn the work. YO and draw lp through the first lp on the hk. YO and draw lp through the next 2 lps on the hook. Continue drawing through 2 lps to end of row.

Step 3: Do not turn the work. Work from right to left. Skip the first vertical lp formed at the edge of the work in previous row. Insert hk from right to left behind the next vertical lp. Yo and draw yarn through the vertical lp. Leave this lp on hook. Continue in this way to end. make sure you do not sk the last vertical lp on left-handed side of work.

Repeat Steps 2 & 3 till project is length called for in pattern.

January 8 Granny's Square Dishcloth

Materials

Off white cotton yarn (400 g/14 oz)

Crochet hook: size 5 mm

Instructions

Ch 5. Join with sl st to form a ring.

1st rnd: Ch 5. (3 dc. Ch 2) 3 times in ring. 2 dc in ring. Join with sl st to 3rd ch of ch 5.

2nd rnd: Sl st in next ch-2 sp. Ch 3 (counts as dc). (2 dc. Ch 2. 3 dc) in same ch-2 sp. [Ch 1. Miss next 3 dc. (3 dc. Ch 2. 3 dc) in next ch-2 sp] 3 times. Ch 1. Join with sl st to top of ch 3.

3rd rnd: Sl st in each of next 2 dc and ch-2 sp. Ch 3 (counts as dc). (2 dc. Ch 2. 3 dc) in same ch-2 sp. [Ch 1. Miss next 3 dc. 3 dc in next ch-1 sp. Ch 1. (3 dc. Ch 2. 3 dc) in next ch-2 sp] 3 times. Ch 1. Join with sl st to top of ch 3.

4th rnd: Sl st in each of next 2 dc and ch-2 sp. Ch 3 (counts as dc). (2 dc. Ch 2. 3 dc) in same ch-2 sp. [(Ch 1. Miss next 3 dc. 3 dc in next ch-1 sp) twice. Ch 1. (3 dc. Ch 2. 3 dc) in next ch-2 sp] 3 times. Ch 1. Miss next 3 dc. 3 dc in next ch-1 sp. Ch 1. Join with sl st to top of ch 3. (Four 3-dc groups on each side of square, including corner groups).

Rep last rnd 4 times more, having 1 more 3-dc group on each side of square on next and every following rnd. Seven 3-dc groups on each side of square.

9th rnd: Ch 1. 1 sc in each dc and 3 sc in corner ch-2 sp around. Join with sl st to first sc. Fasten off.

January 9 Little Starbursts Dishcloth

Materials

Hook size: 5.0 mm

Yarn: Worsted Weight Cotton

Gauge: Finished main body = approx. 18 cm x 18 cm

Instructions

To begin, ch 26.

Row 1: Sc in second ch from hook. Work starburst stitch. *Ch 1. Work starburst stitch.* repeat from * to * across. Sc in same ch.

Row 2-24: Ch 1. Turn. Sc in top of sc. Work starburst stitch. *Ch 1. Work starburst stitch.* repeat from * to * across. Sc in same sc.

January 10 Circle Dishcloths

Materials:

Cotton yarn color of your choice

Size I Crochet Hook.

Instructions:

Base: CH 3

Rnd 1: 8 SC in 1st CH made, SL to 1st SC made, CH 1, turn.

Rnd 2: *SC, CH 1, Rep from* around, SL to 1st SC made, CH 1, turn.

Rnd 3:*SC in CH 1 sp, CH 1, SC in SC sp, CH 1, rep from * around, SL to 1st SC made, CH 1, turn.

Rnd 4-5:*SC in CH 1 sp, CH 1, SK SC sp, Rep from * around, SL to 1st SC made, CH 1, turn.

Rnd 6:*SC in CH 1 sp, CH 1, SC in SC sp, CH 1, rep from * around, Sl to 1st SC made, CH 1, turn.

Rnd 7-9:*SC in CH 1 sp, CH 1, SK SC sp, Rep from * around, Sl to1 st SC sp, CH 1, turn.

Rnd 10:* SC in CH 1 sp, CH 2, SK SC sp, Rep from * around, SL to 1st SC made, CH 1 turn.

Rnd 11-13: SC in CH 2 sp, CH 2, SK Sc sp, Rep from * around, SL to 1st SC made, CH 1, turn,(Rnd 13 Tie off and hide string).

Super Easy and Fun !

January 11 Nubby Dishcloths

Materials:

4mm/size G6 hook.

1 ball (1½ oz) worsted weight cotton.

Instructions

Row 1: Ch 26. Sc in 2nd ch from hook and across. (25)

Row 2: Ch 1, turn. * Sc in first st, tr in next. Repeat from * across, ending with sc.

Row 3: Ch 3, turn. * Sc in tr; tr in next sc. Repeat from * across, ending with tr.

Row 4: Ch 1, turn. * Sc in tr; tr in next sc. Repeat from * across, ending with a sc in top of starting ch 3 of previous row.

Rows 5 to 23: Repeat rows 3 and 4, ending with a row 3. Do not fasten off.

Edging: Ch 1, turn. * Sc across to next corner; 3 sc in last st. Repeat from * around, ending with sl st into first sc. Fasten off and weave ends in.

January 12 Lacy Pearls Dishcloth

Materials: size F hook, 100% Cotton yarn, tapestry needle.

Instructions

Ch 5, join with sl st to form ring.

Rnd 1: Ch 3, 15 dc in ring, join with sl st in top of beg ch 3. (16 dc)

Rnd 2: Ch 4, *dc in next st, ch 1, around, join with sl st in 3rd ch of beg ch 4. (16 ch 1 sp)

Rnd 3: sl st in first ch 1 sp, ch 1, sc in same sp, ch 3, [sc in next ch 1 sp, ch 3] 15 times, join with sl st in first sc. (16 ch 3 sp)

Rnd 4: sl st in first ch 3 sp, ch 1, sc in same sp, ch 3, [sc in next ch 3 sp, ch 3] 15 times, join with sl st in first sc. (16 ch 3 sp)

Rnd 5: sl st in first ch 3 sp, ch 1, sc in same sp, ch 4, [sc in next ch 3 sp, ch 4] 15 times, join with sl st in first sc. (16 ch 4 sp)

Rnd 6: sl st in first ch 4 sp, ch 1, sc in same sp, ch 4, [sc in next ch 4 sp, ch 4] 15 times, join with sl st in first sc. (16 ch 4 sp)

Rnd 7: sl st in first ch 4 sp, ch 1, sc in same sp, ch 5, [sc in next ch 4 sp, ch 5] 15 times, join with sl st in first sc. (16 ch 5 sp)

Rnd 8: sl st in first ch 5 sp, ch 1, sc in same sp, ch 5, [sc in next ch 5 sp, ch 5] 15 times, join with sl st in first sc. (16 ch 5 sp)

Rnd 9: sl st in first ch 5 sp, ch 3, 9 dc in same ch 5 sp, ch 2, sc in next ch 5 sp, ch 2, [10 dc in next ch 5 sp, ch 2, sc in next ch 5 sp, ch 2] 7 times, join with sl st in top of beg ch 3.

Rnd 10: ch 1, sc in same st, ch 3, [sc in next st, ch 3] 8 times, sc in next st, sk next ch 2 sp, sc in next st, sk next ch

2 sp, *[sc in next st, ch 3] 9 times, sc in next st, sk next ch 2 sp, sc in next st, sk next ch 2 sp, repeat from * around, join with sl st in first sc.

Fasten off. Weave in ends.

January 13 Spring Granny Dishcloth

Materials:

Cotton yarn

US Hook size I/5.50mm

Instructions:

Rnd 1: Ch 3, 2 dc in ring, *ch 2, 3 dc, repeat twice from *, join with sl st to 1st dc (ch 3 from beginning of round and throughout pattern). (12 sts)

Rnd 2: Ch 3, 2 dc, [2dc, ch 2, 2dc] in ch 2 sp, *3 dc, [2 dc, ch 2, 2dc] in ch 2 sp, repeat twice from *, join with sl st to 1st dc (ch 3). (28 sts)

Rnd 3: Ch 3, 4 dc, [2dc, ch 2, 2dc] in ch 2 sp, *7 dc, [2dc, ch 2, 2dc] in ch 2 sp, repeat twice from *, 2 dc, join with sl st to 1st dc (ch 3). (44 dc)

Rnd 4: Ch 3, 6 dc, [2dc, ch 2, 2dc] in ch 2 sp, *11 dc, [2dc, ch 2, 2dc] in ch 2 sp, repeat twice from *, 4 dc, join with sl st to 1st dc (ch 3). (60 dc)

Rnd 5: Ch 3, 8 dc, [2dc, ch 2, 2dc] in ch 2 sp, *15 dc, [2dc, ch 2, 2dc] in ch 2 sp, repeat twice from *, 6 dc, join with sl st to 1st dc (ch 3). (76 dc)

Change color

Rnd 6: Ch 3, 10 dc, [2dc, ch 2, 2dc] in ch 2 sp, *19 dc, [2dc, ch 2, 2dc] in ch 2 sp, repeat twice from *, 8 dc, join with sl st to 1st dc (ch 3). (92 dc)

Finish, weave ends. Or continue to optional finish round.

January 14 Easy Ombre Dishcloth

Materials:

Cotton Yarn

Crochet hook: Size 5 mm

Instructions:

Ch 5. Join with sl st to form a ring.

1st rnd: Ch 3 (counts as dc). [3 dc. (Ch 2. 4 dc)] 3 times in ring. Ch 2. Join with sl st to top of ch 3.

2nd rnd: Ch 3 (counts as dc). 1 dc in each of next 3 dc. (2 dc. Ch 2. 2 dc) in next ch-2 sp. *1 dc in each of next 4 dc. (2 dc. Ch 2. 2 dc) in next ch-2 sp. Rep from * twice more. Join with sl st to top of ch 3.

3rd to 8th rnds: Ch 3 (counts as dc). *1 dc in each dc to next ch-2 sp. (2 dc. Ch 2. 2 dc) in next ch-2 sp. Rep from * 3 times more. 1 dc in each dc to end of rnd. Join with sl st to top of ch 3.

9th rnd: Ch 1. 1 sc in each dc around, having 3 sc in corner ch-2 sps. Join with sl st to first sc. Fasten off.

January 15 Baby Ripple Afghan

Materials

Soft Yarn 4(8) oz, Color A, 3(7) oz color B

Size I crochet hook

Instructions

In color A, chain 70(142).

Row 1 : SC into second chain from hook and next 4 chains. *3SC in next chain. SC in next 5 chains. Skip 2 chains. SC in next 5 chains.* Repeat from * to the end. CH1, turn.

Row 2 : Skip first SC. Working in back loops only, SC in next 4 SC. *3SC in next SC. SC in next 5 SC. Skip 2 SC. SC in next 5 SC.* Repeat from * to end. CH1, turn. Attach Color B.

Row 3 : Using Color B, Skip first SC. Working in back loops only, SC in next 4 SC. *3SC in next SC. SC in next 5 SC. Skip 2 SC. SC in next 5 SC.* Repeat from * to end.

Row 4 : Skip first SC. Working in back loops only, SC in next 4 SC. *3SC in next SC. SC in next 5 SC. Skip 2 SC. SC in next 5 SC.* Repeat from * to end. CH1, turn. Drop Color B, pick up Color A.

Rows 5 - 46 (94) : Repeat Rows 3 & 4. End with Color A. For Edging, SC around the edge of the blanket with Color A.

January 16 Glow Thermal Blanket

Materials

Baby yarn

F hook.

Instructions

1.Chain 90,

2.Sc in 3rd chain from the hook.

ch2, sk2, sc in next, to end of row.

ch 1, turn

3.SC first sc, *ch2, sk2, sc in next*.

last stitch of the round is in the first sc of the previous round,

ch1 turn.

repeat round 3 till you have the length that you want.

January 17 Pastel Ripple Baby Blanket

Materials:

100% acrylic yarn

One size US I-9 (5.5 mm) crochet hook

Yarn needle

Row 1: Sc in second ch from hook, sc in next ch, skip 1 ch (edge sts), * sc in next 5 ch, work 3 sc in next ch, sc in next 5 ch, + skip 2 ch; repeat from * across, end last repeat at + skip 1 ch, sc in last 2 ch, turn.

Row 2: Ch 1,working through the back loop only of each st, sc in first 2 sts, skip 1 st, * sc in next 5 sts, work 3 sc in next st, sc in next 5 sts, skip 2 sts; repeat from * 9 times, end sc in next 5 sts, work 3 sc in next st, sc in next 5 sts, skip 1 st, sc in last 2 sts.

Repeat Row 2, following Stripe Sequence, for Ripple patt.

January 18 Poseys In the squares baby blanket

Materials:

100% cotton yarn

Crochet hook: 5.5mm

Yarn needle

Instructions

Square (Make 49)

Ch 3, slip st in first st to form a ring.

Round 1: Ch 3 (counts as dc here and throughout), work 11 dc in ring, slip st in top of beginning ch – 12 sts.

Round 2: Ch 3, [slip st in front loop of next dc, ch 3] around, slip st in back loop in top of beginning ch of Round 1 – 12 loops.

Round 3: Ch 3, 2 dc in same space on Round 1, 3 dc in back loop of next dc on Round 1, ch 3, skip next st, *[3 dc in back loop of next dc] twice, ch 3, skip next st; repeat from * around, slip st in top of beginning ch – 4 ch-3 spaces.

Round 4: Slip st in next dc, ch 3, dc in next 3 dc, skip next dc, (3 dc, ch 3, 3 dc) in ch-3 space, *skip next dc, dc in next 4 dc, skip next dc, (3 dc, ch 3, 3 dc) in ch-3 space; repeat from * around; slip st in back loop of beginning ch.

Round 5: Ch 3, *dc in back loop of each dc to ch-3 space, dc in back loop of next ch, (dc, ch 1, dc) in back loop of next ch, dc in back loop of next ch; repeat from * to last ch-3 space, dc in back loop of next 3 dc, slip st in top of beginning ch.

Round 6: Slip st in front loop of next st on Round 4, ch 1, [slip st in next front loop, ch 1] around, slip st in first slip st.

Fasten off.

January 19 Serene Seaside Square Baby Blanket

Materials:

100% cotton yarn

Crochet hook, 5.5mm

Yarn needle

Instructions:

Squares (Make 36)

Ch 4; join with a slip st to form a ring.

Round 1: Ch 3 (counts as dc), 23 dc in ring; join with a slip st in top of ch 3 – 24 sts.

Round 2: Ch 1, sc in same st as joining, * ch 5, skip next 2 dc, sc in next dc, ch 3, skip 2 dc **, sc in next dc; repeat from * around, end at **; join with a slip st in first sc.

Round 3: (Slip st, ch 3, 2 dc, ch 3, 3 dc) all in first ch-5 space, * 3 dc in ch 3 space **, (3 dc, ch 3, 3 dc) all in next ch-5 space; repeat from * around, end at **; join in top of ch-3.

Round 4: Ch 4 (counts as dc, ch 1), skip next dc, dc in next dc, ch 1, * (dc, ch 3, dc, ch 1) all in ch 3 space **, [dc in next dc, ch 1, skip next dc] 4 times, dc in next dc, ch 1; repeat from * to last 6 dc, end at **; [dc in next dc, ch 1, skip next dc] 3 times; join in 3rd ch of ch 4.

Round 5: Ch 3, [dc in each ch 1 space and dc to corner ch 3 space, (dc, ch 3, dc) all in corner ch 3 space] 4 times, dc in each ch-1 space and dc to end; join in top of ch 3.

Round 6: Ch 1, sc in same st as joining, sc in each dc around and work 5 sc in each corner ch 3 space; join in first sc. Fasten off. Weave in ends.

January 20 Lavender Shell Afghan

Materials:

680 yds. Light Lavender Red Heart 4-ply yarn (L)

310 yds. Petal Pink Red Heart 4-ply yarn (P)

310 yds. White Red Heart 4-ply yarn (W)

H hook or size needed for gauge

Instructions:

Row 1 – With lavender ch 126, sc in 2nd ch from hook, *skip 1 ch, Shell in next ch, skip 1 ch, sc in next ch, rep from * across, sc in last ch, ch 3 and turn. (31 Shells)

Row 2 – Dc in same sp, *sc in center dc of Shell, Shell in next sc, rep from *across ending 2 dc in last sc, ch 1 and turn. (30 Shells)

Row 3 – Sc in same sp, *Shell in next sc, sc in center dc of Shell, rep from * across ending sc in last st, ch 3 and turn.

Row 4 – Rep Row 2 and fasten off.

Row 5 – With pink sc in first dc, continue with Row 3.

Row 6 – Rep Row 2 and fasten off.

January 21 Crochet Baby Blanket

Materials:

Yarn pink in color

Crocket Hook: Size 4 mm

Instructions:

Ch 162.

1st row: (RS). 1 dc in 3rd ch from hook (counts as 2 dc in one ch). Miss next 3 ch. (4 dc. Ch 2. 1 dc) in next ch - Cluster made. *Ch 1. Miss next 3 ch. (1 dc. Ch 1. 1 dc) in next ch – V-st made. Miss next 3 ch. Cluster in next ch. Rep from * to last 4 ch. Ch 1. Miss next 3 ch. 2 dc in last ch.

2nd row: Ch 3. 1 dc in first dc. *Cluster in ch-2 sp of next Cluster. Ch 1. V-st in next V-st. Rep from * to last Cluster. Cluster in ch-2 sp of next

Cluster.

Ch 1. Miss next dc. 2 dc in last dc.

Rep last row for pat until work from beg measures 29 1/2" [75 cm], ending with RS facing for next row. Fasten off.

With RS of work facing, join yarn with sl st to first ch of foundation ch. Ch 3. 1 dc in same sp as sl st (counts as 2 dc). Miss next 3 ch. Cluster in next ch. *Ch 1. Miss next 3 ch. V-st in next ch. Miss next 3 ch. Cluster in next ch. Rep from * 18 times more. Ch 1. Miss next 3 ch. 2 dc in last ch. Fasten off.

January 22 Shells and Stripes Baby Afghan

Materials:

50 yards. 4-ply yarn (pink, blue, yellow and green)

H crochet hook

Instructions:

Row 1 – With pink ch 154 st, Sh St in 7th ch from hook, *skip 3 ch, V St in next ch, skip 3 ch, Sh St in next ch, rep from * across alternating Sh St and V St ending with a Sh St, skip 2 ch, work 1 dc in last ch, ch 3 and turn. (19 Sh St and 18 V St)

Row 2 – V St in first ch 2 sp of Sh St, Sh St in ch 2 sp of V St, rep across alternating V St and Sh St, ending work 1 dc in last dc, ch 3 and turn.

Row 3 – Sh St in first ch 2 sp of V St, V St in next ch 2 sp of Sh St, rep across alternating Sh St and V St, ending work 1 dc in last dc, ch 3 and turn.

Row 4 – Repeat Row 2, fasten off and turn.

Row 5 – Join blue with a sl st in dc, ch 2, Sh St in first V St, V St in next Sh St, rep across alternating Sh St and V St, ending work 1 dc in last dc, ch 3 and turn.

Repeat Rows 2 and 3 having 4 rows in each color as follows:

4 rows pink, 4 rows blue, 4 rows yellow, 4 rows green

Repeat this color sequence 4 times for a total of 64 rows"

January 23 Cuddleworthy Crochet Baby Blanket

Materials:

4.5 mm hook

Cotton yarn 3 balls

Instructions:

Start by making a chain of 105 (Multiples of 6 + 3).

Row 1:

Sc in 2nd ch from hook. Sc in next st. *Ch 4, sk next 4 sts, sc in next 2 sts.* Repeat from * to * across. You should have 2 sc's in last 2 sts.

Rows 2-113:

Ch 1. Turn. Sc in next 2 sts. *Ch 4, sk next 4 ch's, sc in next 2 sc's of previous row.* Repeat from * to * across.

Row 114:

Ch 1. Turn. Sc in next 2 sts. *Ch 4, sk next 4 ch's, sc in next 2 sc's of previous row.* Repeat from * to * across. Fasten Off.

January 24 Blossom Baby Afghan

Materials:

640 yards Hushabye Red Heart 4-ply yarn

385 yards White Red Red Heart 4-ply yarn

50 yards Baby Pink Red Heart 4-ply yarn

40 yards Pale Blue Red Heart 4-ply yarn

40 yards Pale Green Red Heart 4-ply yarn

30 yards Maize Red Heart 4-ply yarn

F, H, and I crochet hook or size needed for gauge

tapestry needle

Instructions

Rnd 1 – With color and H hook ch 2, 8 sc in 2nd ch from hook, join to beg sc.

Rnd 2 – Ch 4, dc in same sp, (dc, ch 1, dc) in each ch around, join to beg ch 3 and fasten off.

Rnd 3 – Join white with a sl st in any ch 1 sp, ch 2, (dc, ch 2, 2 dc) in same sp, *ch 3, sc in next ch 1 sp, ch 3, (2 dc, ch 2, 2 dc) in next ch 1 sp, rep fom * around, join to top of beg ch 2.

Rnd 4 – Sl st into corner ch 2 sp, (sc, ch 3, sc) in same sp, *ch 3, sc in next ch 3 sp (2 times), ch 3, (sc, ch 3, sc) in corner ch 3 sp, rep from * around, join to beg sc and fasten off.

Rnd 5 – With I hook join hushabye with a sl st in any corner ch 3 sp, ch 2, (2 dc, ch 3, 3 dc) in same sp, *3 dc in each ch 3 sp across, (3 dc, ch 3, 3 dc) in corner ch 3 sp, rep from * around, join to top of beg ch 2 and fasten off.

January 25 Baby's First Crochet Baby Blanket Pattern

Materials:

470 yds. White Red Heart 4-ply yarn (A)

340 yds. Petal Pink Red Heart 4-ply yarn (B)

340 yds. Pale Green Red Heart 4-ply yarn (C)

H and I crochet hooks or size needed for gauge

Instructions:

Row 1 – With A and H hook ch 129, Cl in 6th ch from hook, *skip 2 ch, dc in next ch, skip 2 ch, Cl in next ch, rep from * across ending skip 2 ch, dc in last ch, ch 3 and turn.

Row 2 – *Cl in center dc of Cl, skip 2 dc, dc in dc, rep from * across, dc in last dc, fasten off and turn.

Rep Row 2 in a 2-row color pattern:

A, B, C 8 times, finishing 2 rows A (50 rows)

January 26 Bluebell Baby Afghan

Materials:

570 yds. Light Blue Red Heart 4-ply yarn (B)

445 yds. White Red Heart 4-ply yarn (W)

H and I crochet hooks or size needed for gauge

Instructions

Row 1 – With blue ch 124, 2 dc in 5th ch from hook, 2 dc in next ch, *skip 2 ch, 2 dc in each of

next 2 ch, rep from * across ending skip 1 ch, dc in last ch, ch 3 and turn.

Row 2 – Skip 1 dc, 2 dc in each of next 2 dc, *skip 2 dc, 2 dc in each of next 2 dc, rep from *

across, dc in last dc, ch 3 and turn.

Row 3 – Rep Row 2, fasten off and turn.

Row 4 – Join white with a sl st in first dc, ch 2, skip 1 dc, 2 dc in each of next 2 dc, *skip 2 dc,

2 dc in each of next 2 dc, rep from * across, dc in last dc, ch 3 and turn.

January 27 Multiple Use kitchen cloth

Materials:

H Crochet Hook (5.0 mm)

Small amounts of cotton yarn

Tapestry needle for weaving in ends

Instructions

Foundation: Chain 6 and slip stitch into the first chain to form a ring.

Round 1: Make 12 dc into center of ring, join with a sl st to join round.

Round 2: Ch 2, *2 dc into the next stitch, repeat from * to end of round.

Round 3: Ch 2, *1 dc into next stitch, ch 1, repeat from * to end of round.

Round 4: Ch 2 *2 dc into the next stitch, repeat from * to end of round.

Fasten off...

Be creative with the edges as you wish

January 28 Durable Dish Cloth

Materials

Crochet Dish Cloth Pattern

H8/5mm Hook

Instructions

ch 26

Row 1: sc in second stitch from hook and across

Row 2: sc in 1st sc, (ch 1, sk 1 ch, sc) to the end. Ch 1, turn.

Row 3: sc in 1st st (dc in empty ch of row below, sc in next sc) across to end. Ch 1, turn

Row 4: sc in 1st st (ch 1, sk dc, sc in sc) to the end. Ch 1, turn

Row 5: sc in 1st sc (dc in empty space of row below, sc in next sc) across to end. Ch 1, turn

Repeat rows 4 and 5 to the desired size. Mine finished out at 7 3/4" square!

January 29 Heart Hair Decoration

Materials

J hook

Cotton yarn

Instructions

Sh1 Ring 5 - 2 - 2 - 2 - 2 - 2 - 5 close, RW,

Chain 2 - 2 - 2 - 2 - 2 - 1, Lock Join to last picot of ring,

(Chain 1 - 1, Lock Join to next picot on Ring) 2 times,

Chain 1, Sh2 Josephine knot 8, Sh1 Ch 1, Lock Join to next picot on Ring,

(Ch 1 - 1, Lock Join to next picot on Ring) 2 times,

Ch 1 - 2 - 2 - 2 - 2 - 2,

Cut Sh1 thread 14 inches long and hook it up through the space between the Ring and the first Chain.

Now use this cut end as the core thread for a spiral chain if wanted, otherwise fasten off here.

Work two hearts and chains and attach to a hair grip

January 30 Tatted Beaded Earring

Materials

No.80 varigated purple thread

Fish hook

Instructions

String about 15 beads on your shuttle thread.

First Ring:

4 ds, add bead, 4 ds, join to fish hook earring, add bead, 4 ds, add bead, 4 ds. close ring.

Leave 1/8 inch space.

Clover leaf:

4 ds,add bead, 4 ds, add bead,4 ds , p ,4 ds.close ring.

4 ds, join to 3rd p of previous ring , add bead, 4 ds ,add bead , 4 ds , p , 4 ds. close ring.

4 ds, join to p of previous ring, add bead , 4 ds ,add bead ,4 ds, add bead, 4 ds.close ring.

Leave 1/8 inch space. Tie tails and cut. Hide threads.

January 31 Tatted Earring

Material

size 10 Crochet Thread

size 5 Needle

instructions

1st RING 5ds p(bead) 5ds cl rw

2nd RING 5ds p(bead) 5ds cl rw

3rd RING 5ds p(bead) 5ds cl rw <tie a knot here>

4th RING 5ds p(bead) 5ds p 5ds p(bead) 5ds cl <use the picot to hang on earwire

February

February 1: Valentine Heart Earrings

Materials

1 pair of ear wires

size 12 hook

You can use any size thread

Instructions:

1st row: ch 17, sc in 2nd ch from hook and in next 6 ch, skip 2 ch, sc in remaining 7 sc, ch 1 turn.

2nd row: 2 sc in 1st sc, sc in next 6 sc, skip 2 sc, sc in next 6 sc, 2 sc in last sc, ch 1 turn.

3rd row: Same as 2nd row. 4th row: Same as 2nd row.

5h row: sc in next 6 sc, skip 2 sc, sc in remaining 6 sc, ch 1 turn.

6th row: sc in next 5 sc, skip 2 sc, sc in remaining 5 sc, ch 1 DO NOT TURN.

Attach to ear wires.

February 2: Amigurumi Heart

Materials

Crochet hook No.1 (2,25 mm)

Red cotton yarn

Polyfil

Tapestry needle and scissors

Rnd 1: Work 6 sc into the center of ring (6)

Rnd 2: Work 2 sc in each st around (12)

Rnd 3: (Sc in next st, 2 sc in next st) around (18)

Sl st in next st, cut yarn leaving 10" long tail and pull through last loop. You've just finished the first top half of the heart .

Repeat Rnd 1-3 for second half of heart

Do not cut yarn.

Rd 4 : Sc in next 9 sts

Merge the halves together: Insert hook into first stitch after sl st and continue to make 1 sc in all 18 stitches. Insert hook back into second half and work 1 sc in next 9 sc. (One round completed with 36 sc)

With the tail close the gap between the two top halves.

Rd 5 : Sc around (36)

Rd 6 : (Sc in next 4 sts, sc2tog) around (30)

Rd 7: (Sc in next 3 sts, sc2tog) around (24)

Rd 8: (Sc in next 2 sts, sc2tog) around (18)

Rd 9: (Sc in next st, sc2tog) around (12)

Stuff and remember not to leave the tail inside

Continue with "sc in next st, sc2tog" until you heave 5 sts left.

Cut yarn and pull it through the last loop. Now pull the top tail tight to shape the heart and hide the tail inside with tapestry needle.

With a tapestry needle, weave the tail through the front loops of the remaining 5 stitches and pull it tight to close. Weave in yarn end!

February 3: Sweetheart Earrings

Materials

Yarn - red crochet cotton

Hook – 1.5 mm.

Notions – earring hooks.

Instruction

Make 4 ch.

1st round: 11 tr into 1st of the 4 ch. The other 3 ch count as first tr. Sl st into top of 3ch to join round.

2nd round: sl st into next tr, (1 dc {US = sc}, 2 tr) into next tr, (2 tr, 1 dc) into next tr, sl st into next tr, (1dc, 2 tr) into next tr, (2 tr, 1 dc) into next tr, sl st into next 3 tr, (1 dc, 1 tr, 1 dc) into next tr, sl st into next 3 tr. Fasten off.

Tie loose ends.

Attach earring hooks to the back loop only of the sl st at the center of the top of the heart.

February 4: Valentine's Crochet Heart

Materials

Yarn   1 skein

Mercerised cotton 160m/50g

175 yards/1,76 ounces

For starching ½ cup potato starch   ½ cup cold water   ½ cup warm water   plastic foil

Hook   7 mm

Sewing needle

Instructions

Round 1   Chain 3, 10 dc in ring, 1 sl st in 3rd beginning chain.

Round 2   Chain3; 2 dc in next stitch 10 times; 1 sl st in 3rd beginning chain.

Round 3   Chain 1, 2 sc;[2 trebles in next stitch] 2 times; [2 dc in next stitch] 3 times; 2 sc; [2 sc in next stitch] 2 times; 2 sc, [2 dc in next stitch] 3 times; [2 trebles in next stitch] 2 times; 2 sc; 1 sl st in this rows 1st chain.

Round 4   Chain 1, 1 sc; [2 trebles in next stitch] 2 times; [2 dc, 2 dc in next stitch] 3 times; 2 dc, 4 trebles, 2 dc; [2 dc in next stitch, 2 dc] 3 times; [2 trebles in next stitch] 2 times; 1 sc, 1 sl st in this rows 1st chain.

Weave in the ends

February 5: Crochet Heart

Materials

Cotton Yarn

7 mm hook

Instructions

Round 1: Chain 2, 15 dc into ring, sl st into top of first dc.

Round 2: Chain 2, 1 dc into same stitch, 4 trc into next stitch, 2 dc into next stitch, 1 hdc into each of next four stitches.

For the bottom part; 1 dc, 1 trc, 1 dc into next stitch.

Turn over

1 hdc into each of next four stitches, 2 dc into next stitch, 4 trc into next stitch, 1 dc into next stitch, chain 2, sl st into same stitch.

Fasten off, pull magic ring closed, weave in ends.

February 6: American Folk-Art Heart Motif

Materials:

Worsted Weight Yarn

H/8-5.00 MM Hook

Instructions

Ch. 14.

Dc in 4th ch from hook, dc in next 4 ch, 3 dc in next ch, dc in next 5 ch. Ch 3 and make sl st in bottom of beginning ch (the one in which you just made a dc st). Turn and ch 3.

Dc 7 in ch3 space. Dc in next 6 dc, 3 dc in next dc, dc in next 6 dc, dc 7 in ch3 space. Dc in bottom of next 4 ch, dc3tog over next 3 ch, dc in bottom of next 3 ch and sl st in top of ch3 (turning ch). Turn and ch 3.

Dc in next 2 dc, dc3tog over next 3 dc, dc in next 4 dc. 2 dc in each of next 5 dc, dc in next 8 dc, 5 dc in next dc, dc in next 8 dc, 2 dc in each of next 5 dc, dc in next dc, sl st in top of ch3 (turning ch). Finish off.

February 7: Valentine's Day Basket

Materials:

Size J Crochet Hook

Size H Crochet

Worsted Weight Yarn

Tapestry Needle

Instructions:

MC

10 sc into MC. Join into first sc. Ch 2. (10)

2 dc into each st around. Join. Ch 2. (20)

1 dc into next st, 2 dc into next st Repeat around. Join. Ch 2. (30)

1 dc into next 2 sts, 2 dc into next st Repeat around. Join. Ch 2. (40)

Dc into each st around. Join. Ch 2. (40)

Start your basket weave stitch: *fpdc in the next 4 sts, bpdc in the next 4 sts* Repeat around. Join. Ch 2 (40)

bpdc in the next 4 sts, fpdc in the next 4 sts Repeat around. Join. Ch 2 (40)

Repeat steps 7 and 8 for the next 2 rounds

hdc in each st around. Join. Ch 2. (40)

hdc in each st around. Join.

Now for the handle: Ch 25 (if you want a longer handle, chain a longer ch) Sk 19 sts. Sl st into 20th st. Ch 1. Sc into second ch from hook and into each ch across. Sc into the hdc from the previous round. Fasten off and weave ends.

February 8 Beautiful Heart Design

Materials

DK yarn

4mm crochet hook

Wool needle

Toy stuffing

Stitch holder

Instructions

Row 1 - 6SC into magic ring (6)

Row 2- INC around (12)

Row 3- "1SC INC" around (18)

Row 4- "2SC INC" around (24)

Cut yarn and leave working loop on a stitch holder

Repeat instructions above to create the second circle

Joining the circles

SC in the next ST on the first circle; SC working round the 23 stitches of the first circle

Round 23 stitches of the second circle.

*That gap in the middle is normal.

Row 6- SC around (46)

Row 7- 21SC DEC twice (44)

Row 8- "9SC DEC" around (40)

Row 9- "8SC DEC" around (36)

Row 10- "4SC DEC" around (30)

Row 11-end "3SC DEC" around

Stuff the heart as you go

Bind off and cut yarn

Close the gaps with a needle

February 9: Cold Heart Snowflake

Materials:

Size 10 crochet thread

Size 4 crochet hook

Empty pizza box

Wax paper or foil

Cellophane tape, glue, water, glitter, small container for glue/water mixture, pins

Instructions

Make magic ring.

Round 1: Ch 3, 11 dc in ring, sl st in 3rd ch of starting ch. Pull magic circle tight.

Round 2: *Ch 15 (this will later form ch 3 and 1st half of heart), sl st in 2nd ch from hook, sc in next ch (this will form inside point of heart), ch 9 (this will form 2nd half of heart), sl st in 4th ch of starting ch 15, ch 3, sk 1 dc, sl st in next dc; repeat from * around 5 times, sl st in starting sl st.

Round 3: *Into next ch 3 work 3 sc and 1 sl st; into 1st half of heart work 1 sl st, 5 sc, 2 hdc, 3 dc, 3 hdc and 4 sc, skip over inside point of heart and in 2nd half of heart work 4 sc (pull tight on 1st sc to complete inside heart point), 3 hdc, 3 dc, 2 hdc, 5 sc and 1 sl st, into next ch 3 work 1 sl st and 3 sc; repeat from * around 5 times, sl st in starting sc; bind off. Weave in ends.

Finish: Tape wax paper or foil to top of empty pizza box. Pin snowflake to box on top of wax paper or foil.

February 10: Coaster colored hearts

Materials:

Size 10 crochet thread

Size 1 steel hook

Instructions

Ch 8, join with sl st to form ring

Rnd 1: sl st in ring, ch 3, dc in ring, ch 1, (2 dc in ring, ch 1) 8x, join w/ sl st to 3rd beg ch; 9 ch-sps

Rnd 2: sl st in 1st dc and in 1st ch-sp, ch 3, 2 dc in same sp, ch 2, (3 dc in next ch sp, ch 2) around, join w/ sl st to 3rd beg ch; 9 ch-sps

Rnd 3: sl st in next 2 dc, and in 1st ch-sp, ch 3, (2 dc, ch 1, 3 dc) in same ch-sp, ch 1, (work shell in next ch-sp, ch 1) around, join w/ sl st to 3rd beg ch; 9 shells

Finish off

Rnd 4: using contrasting color, join w/ dc in ch-sp of any shell, tr, dtc, ch 2, dtc, tr, dc, ch 4, (dc, tr, dtc, ch 2, dtc, tr, dc, ch 4) in ea shell around; 9 "peaks" – these will be the hearts

Finish off

Rnd 5: using main color, working in front of ch-4 sps from Rnd 4, join w/ dc in any unused ch-sp from Rnd 3, * dc in next st, tr in next st, ch 4, bringing the ch behind the "peaks," sk 1st st after peak, tr in next st, dc, dc in ch-sp, rep from * around, join with sl st to starting dc

NOTE: all ch-4 sps should be on wrong side of work, they should not be visible from front of finished piece

Rnd 6: ch 3, 2 dc in same st, * work shell in ch 2 of Rnd 4, sk tr and next dc on Rnd 5, 3 dc in next dc, rep from * around, work last shell as prev, join with sl st to 3rd beg ch

Finish off

February 11: Chains of Hearts Crochet Bracelet

Materials

1 pc 5.0-cm extender chain

1 pc 1.0-cm lobster lock

2 pcs 1.0-cm metal rings

Small amount of yarn in two complementing colors

Suitable crochet hook

Tapestry needle

Plarn

Instructions

To make a heart chain:

Round 1: [Ch 9, sk 2 ch, (hdc, 3 dc, hdc) in next ch, sk 1 ch, sl st, sk 1 ch, (hdc, 3 dc, hdc) in next ch, sk 1 ch, sl st. In ch where this sl st was made, (tr, 2dc, tr, 2dc, tr) sl st in 8th ch of ch-9] one heart made. Repeat Round 1 to make a heart chain. Break off and weave in ends.

Pass plarn underneath previous heart chain, YO, pull yarn through.

Work the next heart on the other side of the heart chain to achieve an alternate colored hearts bracelet and repeat to the end

Assemble the Bracelet

February 12: Feel the Love Coaster

Materials

4ply yarn and I hook - 4 1/2 x 5 1/2"

Instructions

ch 8, sl st in 1st ch to form ring

Round 1 - ch2 (counts as 1st dc) and 16 more dc in ring, sl st into top of ch2 to join (17 dc)

Row 2 - ch1, turn, (sc, ch2) in same dc, (hdc, ch1) in next 2 sts, (sc, ch1) in next 5 sts, (sc, ch1, twice) in next st, (sc, ch1) in next 5 sts, (hdc, ch1) in next 3 sts, do not join

Round 3 - turn, (sc, ch1) in next ch-sp, (hdc, ch1) in next ch-sp, (dc, ch1) in next 2 ch-sps, (hdc, ch1) in next 4ch-sps, (dc, ch1, twice) in next ch-sp, (hdc, ch1) in next 4 ch-sps, (dc, ch1) in next 2 ch sps, (hdc, ch1) in next sp, sc in last ch-sp, sl st into top of (sc,ch1), ch2, sc in sp between the top 2 dcs of the first Round, ch1, sl st into 1st ch1

Round 4 -Do NOT turn, ch4, hdc, in ch-sp, (ch3, hdc) in next 2 ch-sps, (ch3, sc) in next 5 ch-sps, for picot in bottom point - (ch4, sc in 3rd ch from hook, ch1), skip next 2 dcs, (sc, ch3) in next 5 ch-sps, (hdc, ch3) in next 2 ch-sps, (hdc, ch4) in sc, slst between the 2dcs of the 1st Round, ch3, sl st into base of the first ch-4 sp

Round 5 - Do NOT turn, ch3, (sc ch3 twice) in next ch-4 sp, (sc, ch3) in next 7 ch-3 sps, (sc, ch3 twice) in center of picot, (sc, ch3) in next 7 ch-3 sps, (sc, ch3, twice) in last ch sp, sl st into sl st, and sl st into the first ch coming out of the sl st to finish.

Tie off and weave in ends.

February 13: Crochet small heart

Materials

H hook

White Red Yarn

Yarn needle

Instructions

Rnd 1. Ch 2, work 7 hdc in the 2nd chain from the hook, sl st.

Rnd 2. Ch 1, work 5 DC in the 1st hdc, 2 hdc in the next hdc, 2 hdc in the next hdc, 2 DC in the next hdc, 2 hdc in the next hdc, 2 hdc in the next hdc, 5 DC in the last hdc, Ch 1, sl st. Fasten off, Weave in the ends.

February 14: Floral heart motif

Materials

Worsted weight cotton or cotton-blend yarn:

Crochet hook size G

Tapestry needle

Instructions

Beginning treble crochet cluster (beg tr cl): Ch 3, holding back last lp of each tr on hook, work 2 tr in same place as ch 3, yo, draw through all 3 lps on hook.

Treble crochet cluster (tr cl): Holding back last lp of each tr on hook, work 3 tr in place indicated, yo, draw through all 4 lps on hook.

Motif

With pink, ch 5, join in beginning ch to form ring.

Rnd 1: Ch 1, work 12 sc in ring, join in beg sc. (12 sc)

Rnd 2: Beg tr cl in same sc as joining, [ch 3, tr cl in next sc] 11 times, ch 3, join in top of beg tr cl, fasten off. (12 tr cl)

Rnd 3: Join white in any ch-3 sp, ch 1, (sc, ch 1, hdc, ch 1, dc, ch 1, tr, ch 1) in same sp, (dtr, ch 1) 4 times in next ch-3 sp, (tr, ch 1) twice in next ch-3 sp, (dc, ch 1) twice in next ch-3 sp, (hdc, ch 1, dc, ch 1) in next ch-3 sp, (dc, ch 1, tr, ch 1) in next ch-3 sp, (tr, ch 1, dc, ch 1) in next ch-3 sp, (dc, ch 1, hdc, ch 1) in next ch-3 sp, (dc, ch 1) twice in next ch-3 sp, (tr, ch 1) twice in next ch-3 sp, (dtr, ch 1) 4 times in next ch-3 sp, (tr, ch 1, dc, ch 1, hdc, ch 1, sc, ch 1) in last ch-3 sp, join in beg sc.

Rnd 4: Sl st over next ch 1, hdc and ch 1, sc in each rem st and ch-1 sp to the ch-1 sp between the 2 tr at bottom point, work (dc, ch 1, dc) in ch-1 sp at point, sc in each rem st and ch-1 sp, ending with sl st over last hdc, ch 1 and sc, join, fasten off.

Rnd 5: Join pink with a sc in the ch-1 sp between the beginning and ending scs of rnd 3 at top center of heart, ch 3, sc in sl st worked over the first hdc of rnd 3, [ch 3, sk next st, sc in next st] around, at bottom point working sc in the first dc, ch 3, sc in next dc, end with ch 3, join in beg sc, fasten off.

February 15: Arch Bracelet

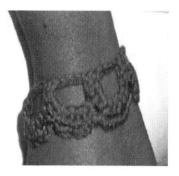

Materials:

Fine Weight Yarn

Crochet Hook 2.25 mm C

Bracelet Clasp

Jump Rings

Crochet yarn size 2

Instructions

Row 1: ch 33, sc in second ch from hook, sc in next ch, (ch 7, skip 3 ch, sc in next 2 sc) across: 56 sts

Row 2: ch 1, turn, sc in first 2 sc, (7 sc in next ch-space, sc2tog) 5 times, 7 sc in next ch-space, sc in last 2 sc: 51 sc

Row 3: ch 3, turn, skip first 3 sc, (sc in next sc, [ch 3, skip 1 sc, sc in next sc] 2 times, ch 1, skip 3 sc) 5 times, sc in next sc, (ch 3, skip 1 sc, sc in next sc) 2 times, ch 3, skip 2 sc, sc in last sc: 63 sts

Finish off.

February 16: Martis Bracelets

Materials:

Cotton yarn in red and white

2.5 mm crochet hook

Scissors

Beads

Instructions

Row 1: Holding white yarn make a chain of 50. Cut a long yarn tail. At the end of your yarn tail start adding 50 beads.

Row 2: Sc in secod chain from hook by pushing your beads so that you can actually crochet over them. Continue to the end, fasten off and weave in ends. Done!

February 17: Crochet Beaded Bracelet

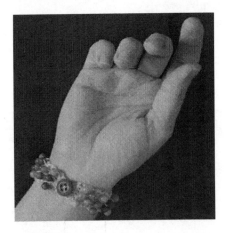

Materials

Crochet Cotton Thread

48 beads

1 button

Big-holed needle

Size C crochet hook

Instructions

Thread 48 beads on crochet cotton thread.

ch 7, leaving about 10" of crochet cotton thread before the start of the chain.

Row 1 - Starting with 2nd ch from hook, sc in each of the next 6 ch, ch 1, turn.

Row 2 - sc in each stitch across (total 6), ch 1, turn.

Row 3 - sc in each stitch across (total 6), ch 1, turn.

Row 4 - sc, bsc, sc, bsc, sc, bsc, ch 1, turn.

Row 5 - sc in each stitch across (total 6), ch 1, turn.

Row 6 - 2 sc, bsc, sc, bsc, sc, ch 1, turn.

Row 7 - repeat Rows 3-6 until you've used all the beads.

Last Row - sc in each stitch across (total 6), ch 3, turn.

Button Hole - skip 5 stitches, sc in last stitch of previous row, finish off, weave in end.

Attach button with 10" thread at beginning of bracelet and weave in end.

February 18: Tunisian Check Scrubbie

Materials:

Medium Weight Yarn

Crochet Hook J (6.0 mm)

Crochet yarn size 4

Instructions

Row 1: ch 13, pull up a loop in second ch from hook and in each ch across

Return Pass: (yarn over, pull through 2 loops on hook) across: 12 TSS

Rows 2-5: tks in first 4 sts, tps in next 4 sts, tks in last 4 sts: 12 sc

Rows 6-9: tps in first 4 sts, tks in next 4 sts, tps in last 4 sts: 18 sc

Rows 10-13: Repeat rows 2-5

Finish off.

February 19: Honey Earrings

Materials:

Size 10 Thread

Crochet Hook E (3.5 mm)

Earwires

2 Beads (about 6 mm)

Instructions

String beads onto the thread

Row 1: ch with bead, ch 1, sc in second ch from hook: 1 sc

Row 2: ch 4, turn, sl st in sc: 4 ch

Row 3: ch 1, turn, 10 sc in ch-space: 10 sc

Row 4: turn, (ch 4, skip 1 sc, sl st in next sc) 5 times: 20 sts

Row 5: ch 1, turn, 5 sc in each of next 5 ch-spaces: 25 sc

Finish off.

February 20: Flower Applique

Materials:

Medium Weight Yarn

Crochet hook G (4.00 mm)

Crochet yarn size 4

Instructions

Round 1: ch 2, 6 sc in second ch from hook, sl st in first sc: 6 sc

Round 2: (make 2 knots, 2 sc in next sc) around: 12 sc, 12 knots

Finish off, and weave in ends.

February 21: Pendant Necklace

Materials:

Size 3 Crochet Thread

Crochet hook US 1 (2.35 mm)

Chain

1 Clasp

2 – 4 Jump rings

Pliers

Crochet yarn size 1

Instructions

Row 1: ch 33, working in back ridge only, dc in fourth ch from hook and in next 13 ch, 4 dc in next ch, dc in next 15 ch: 34 dc

Row 2 – 3: ch 3, turn, skip first 2 dc, dc in next 14 dc, 2 dc in each of next 2 dc, dc in next 14 dc, skip 1 dc, dc in last dc: 34 dc

Finish off.

Attach chain to top corners of pendant with jump rings and pliers. Attach clasp to chain.

February 22: Bead Stripped Poach

Materials:

Size 10 Thread

40 beads in each of 3 colors

Crochet Hook C (2.75 mm)

Crochet yarn size 0

Instructions

String beads – top color should be strung first, bottom color should be strung last.

Round 1: ch 13, working in back loops only, dc in forth ch from hook and in each ch across, working into front loops on opposite side of chain, dc in next 10 ch, sl st in first dc: 20 dc

Round 2: ch 4, turn, dtr with beads in first 10 dc, dtr in next 10 dc, sl st in first dc: 20 dtr

Round 3: ch 3,turn, dc in each dtr around, sl st in first dc: 20 dc

Round 4 – 7: Repeat rows 2-3

Finish off.

February 23: Adria Earrings

Materials:

Size 10 thread

Crochet Hook E (3.5 mm)

Earwires

Instructions

Round 1: make adjustable ring, 24 dc in ring, tighten ring but do not close completely, sl st in first dc: 24 dc

Round 2: ch 3, (dc in next 2 dc, fpdc in next dc) around: 24 dc

Round 3: ch 2, (hdc in next 2 dc, fphdc in next dc) around: 24 hdc

Finish off. Attach earwires.

February 24: Chic Pincushion

Materials:

Sport Weight Yarn

Crochet Hook E (3.50 mm)

Stitch marker

Yarn Needle

Eyes or Buttons

Scrap of Yellow or Orange Fabric

3″ (7.5 cm) Foam Ball

Crochet yarn size 2

Instruction

Round 1: make adjustable ring, ch 3, 12 dc in ring, sl st in first dc: 12 dc

Round 2: ch 3, 2 dc in each dc around, sl st in first dc: 24 dc

Round 3: ch 3, (2 bpdc in next dc, bpdc in next dc) around, sl st in first dc: 36 bpdc

Round 4 – 9: ch 3, dc in each dc around, sl st in first dc: 36 dc

Put foam ball in chick before starting to decrease.

Round 10: ch 3, (dc2tog, dc in next dc) around, sl st in first dc: 24 dc

Round 11: ch 3, dc2tog around, sl st in first dc: 12 dc

Round 12: ch 3: dc2tog around, sl st in first dc: 6 dc

Finish off. Weave end through tops of the stitches and draw closed.

Left Wing

Round 1: make adjustable ring, ch 1, 6 sc in ring, place marker: 6 sc

Round 2: 2 sc in each sc around: 12 sc

Round 3: (2 sc in next sc, sc in next sc) around: 18 sc

Round 4: ch 2, turn, 2 sc in second ch from hook, sc in each sc around: 20 sc

Finish off. Use end to attach wing to body.

Right Wing:

Round 1: make adjustable ring, ch 1, 6 sc in ring, place marker: 6 sc

Round 2: 2 sc in each sc around: 12 sc

Round 3: (2 sc in next sc, sc in next sc) around: 18 sc

Round 4: ch 1, turn, sc in each sc around, 2 fsc increase: 20 sc

Finish off. Use end to attach wing to body.

February 25: Pearly Heart Charm

Materials:

0.5 mm clear beading cord

Steel Crochet Hook 6 (1.8 mm)

12 seed beads (size 11)

1 glass pearl (4 mm)   crochet yarn size 0

Instructions

String red seed beads first then pearl.

Row 1: ch 1 with pearl, 5 sc in chain: 5 sc

Row 2: ch 1, turn, 2 sc in each of next 2 sc, 3 sc in next sc, 2 sc in each of next 2 sc: 11 sc

Row 3: ch 1, turn, (sc with bead, sc) in first 5 sc, (sc with bead, sc, sc with bead) in next sc, (sc, sc with bead) in last 5 sc: 23 sc

Finish off.

February 26: Bumps and Ridges Wash-cloth

Materials:

Medium Weight Yarn (approximately 25 yards)

Crochet Hook J (6.00 mm)

Instructions

Row 1: ch 24, hdc in third ch from hook and in each ch across: 22 hdc

Row 2: ch 2, turn, fphdc in first hdc, bphdc in next 20 hdc, fphdc in last hdc: 22 hdc

Row 3: ch 2, turn, bphdc in first hdc, hdc in next 20 hdc, bphdc in last hdc: 22 hdc

Row 4: ch 2, turn, fphdc in first hdc, (hdc in next 2 hdc, bobble, hdc in next 2 hdc) 4 times, fphdc in last hdc: 22 sts

Row 5: repeat row 3

Row 6 – 17: Repeat rows 2-5

Row 18: Repeat row 2

Finish off.

February 27: Sparkly Beaded Crochet Bracelet

Materials

Metallic crochet thread

Beads with large holes for crochet thread

Clasp

Crochet hook 3.5 mm

Instructions

Crochet a long enough chain, the size of your wrist

Row 1: SK CH1, SC to end of the row; CH1, Turn

Row 2: Thread the beads to the crochet thread. Pull a bead close to work, SC in the next stitch; Repeat to the end

Finish Off: Tie the crochet thread to each end and attach a clasp. Tie off and weave the ends.

February 28: Beaded Bangles

Materials:

Super Fine Weight yarn

Crochet Hook F (3.75 mm)

3 1/4" craft band

25 seed beads

Instructions

Row 1: string 25 beads onto the yarn.

Make a slip knot to the front of the band

Pull up a lp and ch 1 over ring, *6 sc into ring,

Pull a bead up close to the hook, ch 1 with bead

Push the bead up to make sure it is visible, repeat from * until you have used all the beads or the band is wrapped as tightly as desired,

sl st to beginning sc: 150 sc

Finish off.

March

March 1 Tatted Earring

Material

size 10 Crochet Thread and a size 5 Needle

Instructions

1st RING 10ds p(bead) 10ds cl rw

2nd RING 20ds p(bead) 10ds cl leave a small loop to hang ear wire

March 2 Small Tatted Earring

Material

size 10 Crochet Thread and a size 5 Needle

Instructions

1st RING 5ds p(bead) 5ds p(bead) 5ds p(bead) 5ds p(bead) 5ds cl rw

2nd RING 2ds p 2ds cl use the picot to hang ear wire

March 3 Tatted Earring Pattern

Material

size 10 Crochet Thread and a size 5 Needle

make the bottom wings first

Instructions

Bottom wings:

1st RING 5ds p(bead) 2ds p(bead) 3ds tiny p 2ds cl rw

2nd RING 5ds p(bead) 2ds p(bead) 3ds tiny p 2ds cl rw

Top wings:

3rd RING 2ds join to tiny p 5ds p(bead) 2ds p 2ds p(bead) 7ds cl rw

4th RING 2ds join to tiny p 5ds p(bead) 2ds p 2ds p(bead) 7ds cl rw

hang ear wire on the picot

March 4 Cute Girly Earring

Material

size 10 Crochet Thread and a size 5 Needle

Instruction

1st RING 2ds p 2ds p 2ds p 2ds p 2ds p 2ds p 2ds cl rw

2nd RING 4ds p(bead) 4ds p(bead) 4ds p 4ds p(bead) 4ds p(bead) 4ds cl

use the picot to hang ear wire

March 5 Crochet Earring

Material

size 10 Crochet Thread and a size 5 Needle

this one uses 8 small beads i used pearls on this pair.

Instructions

Chain 15ds rw leaving a small loop on end to hang ear wire.

Ring 1ds p(bead) 2ds p(bead) 2ds p(bead) 2ds p(bead) 2ds p(bead) 2ds p(bead) 2ds p(bead) 2ds p(bead) 1ds cl

tie knots use the loop left on top to hang ear wire.

March 6 Tatted Earring

Material

size 10 Crochet Thread and a size 5 Needle

Instructions

1st RING 6ds p(bead) 6ds p(bead) 6ds p(bead) 6ds cl rw

2nd RING 6ds p(bead) 6ds p 6ds p(bead) 6ds cl

Tie knots

March 7 Jewel Earring

Material

size 10 Crochet Thread and a size 5 Needle

Instructions

1st ring 5ds p(bead) p(bead) p(bead) 5ds cl rw

2nd ring 5ds p 5ds cl

Use picot to hang ear wire

March 8 Tatted Earring

Material

size 10 Crochet Thread and a size 5 Needle

6mm beads, 2 per earring.

Instructions

Chain Bead 10ds rw Bead 10ds rw

Ring 2ds p 2ds cl

Tie knots

March 9 Decorative Letter I

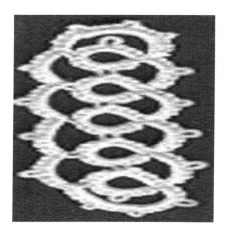

Materials

No. 20 Crochet Cotton

Shuttle and ball thread - do not cut shuttle from ball.

Hook for joining

Instructions

5 cm high and 1.5 cm wide

R 4 DS, 3 P sep by 4 DS, 4 DS, cl. R, RW.

C 4 DS, P, 4 DS, RW.

R 4 DS, J to last P of previous R, 4 DS, 2 P sep by 4 DS, 4 DS, cl. R, RW.

Repeat 2 and 3 four times in total - five Rs and 4 Cs in the row.

C 4 DS, 3 P sep by 4 DS, 4 DS, lock J to centre P of last R, do not RW.

C 4 DS, P, 4 DS, lock J to free P of next R, do not RW. Repeat this C 4 times in total.

C 4 DS, 3 P sep by 4 DS, 4 DS, fasten to base of 1st R and finish ends.

March 10 Spring Flowers Bookmark

Materials

Ball thread 1 shuttle

No. 8 crochet

Instructions

R10-5 cl.

R5+5-5 cl.

R5+10 cl. RW.

R6-6 cl. RW.

Ch 15. RW.

Second flower:

Same as previous flower(s), except the first ring: (R5+5-5 cl.).

Continue until length required.

Make a chain of 5ds, rw, 5ds, rw, 5ds, rw, 5ds etc. and attach a tassel or charm to the end.

March 11 Floral Bookmark Tatting Pattern

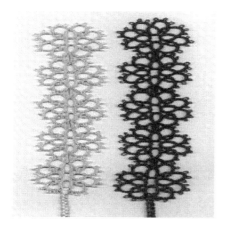

Material

1 shuttle and ball thread

Crochet hook of your choice

Instructions

Large Ring: 7 p 3 p 4 p 3 p 7. cl r, rw.

**Chain: 4 p 3 p 3 p 4. rw

Small Ring: 5 j (to last p of Large Ring) 2 p 5. cl r, rw

Large Ring: 7 j (to last p of Small Ring) 3 j (to 3rd p of Large Ring) 4 p 3 p 7. cl r, rw.

Repeat from ** once more.

Chain: 8 rw.

March 12 Beginners 2 Strand Crochet Afghan Pattern

Materials

48 ounces worsted weight yarn

Size P hook

Instructions

Row 1: Ch 79, sc in second ch from hook and each ch across (78 sc)

Row 2: Ch 3 turn, skip first sc, dc in each sc across.

Row 3: Ch 1 turn, sc in each dc across, sc in top of ch 3.

Rep rows 2 and 3 until desired length.

Ch 1, do not turn, sc in evening along edging with 3 sc in each corner. Join with sl st to first sc. Fasten off yarn. Weave in ends.

March 13 Summer Coaster

Materials

5.50mm hook

Worsted weight yarn in your choice of colors (3 colors, A, B and C)

Instructions

With Color A, ch 58 loosely.

Row 1: Sc in the second ch from hook. *Sc in next st, then hdc in next 2 sts, dc in next 2 sts, tr in next 3 sts, dc in next 2 sts, hdc in next 2 sts, sc in next 2 sts. Repeat from * to end of row. (57 sts)

Row 2: Ch1 and turn. Sc in ea st across to end. (57 sc)

Row 3: With Color B, ch 4 and turn. Work this row and all remaining odd numbered rows in BLO, except for the very last st of the row. *Tr in next st, dc in next 2 sts, hdc in next 2 sts, sc in next 3 sts, hdc in next 2 sts, dc in next 2 sts, tr in next 2 sts. Repeat from * to end of row. (57 sts)

Row 4: Ch1 and turn. Sc in ea st across to end. (57 sc)

Rows 5 – 30: Repeat Rows 1 – 4 6x, and then repeat Rows 1 – 2 once more. Use Color C for Rows 23 – 24 if desired. Break yarn and finish off.

March 14 Crochet Button Earrings

Materials

US-2 steel hook (2.2 mm)

Fingering weight yarn

Yarn Needle

Scissors

Hot glue

2 – 1" or 1.25" buttons

2 – 7 mm jump rings

2 – Fish Hook Earrings

Instructions

Ch 2

Rnd 1 – work 6sc in 2nd ch from hk. (6)

Rnd 2 – work 2sc in each st around. (12)

Rnd 3 – sc in first, 2sc in next, (sc in next, 2sc in next) around, join with slst to first sc of rnd. (18)

Fasten off and leave a 12" tail. Make a total of 4 little circles.

March 15 Flamingo Seat Cover

Materials

100% cotton yarn

Crochet Hook No. 9.

Make a chain 12 inches long.

1st row: Sc in 2nd ch from hook and in each ch across until row measures 8 inches, having an uneven number of sc. Cut off remaining chain. Ch 2, turn.

2nd row: Tr in first sc, * sc in next sc, tr in next sc. Repeat from * across. Ch 1, turn.

3rd row: 2 sc in first st, sc in each st across, 2 sc in last st. Ch 2, turn.

Repeat 2nd and 3rd rows alternately until piece measures 6 inches.

Work in pattern without increasing for 3 more inches. Now dec 1 sc at beginning and end of each sc row until piece measures 14½ inches, ending with a tr row—to dec 1 sc, work off 2 sc as 1 sc. Break off.

March 16 Bath Mat

Materials

24 balls of cotton yarn

Crochet Hook No. 2/0

Instructions

Starting at narrow end, ch 131 to measure 22 inches.

1st row: Sc in 2nd ch from hook and in each ch across. Ch 4, turn.

2nd row: Picking up back loop only, skip first sc, tr in each sc across. Ch 1, turn.

3rd row: Insert hook in back loop of first tr and in free loop of first sc on preceding row, sc in same place, * make an sc through back loop of next tr and free loop of next sc.

Repeat from * across. Ch 1, turn.

4th and 5th rows: Sc in each sc across. Ch 1, turn. At end of 5th row, ch 4, turn.

Repeat 2nd to 5th rows incl until piece measures 34 inches, ending with 3rd row.

March 17 Classic Bath Mat

Materials

100% cotton yarn

Crochet Hook No. 2/0

Starting at bottom, ch 133 to measure 22 inches.

1st row: Sc in 2nd ch from hook, sc in each ch across. Ch 3, turn.

2nd row: Holding all loops back on hook, thread over, insert hook in first sc, * draw thread through and up to height of work, thread over, insert hook in same sc, draw thread through and up to height of work, holding all loops on hook, skip next sc, thread over, insert hook in next sc, draw thread through and up to height of work, thread over, insert hook in same sc, draw thread through and up to height of work, thread over and draw through all loops on hook, ch 1 to fasten (joint puff st made), thread over, insert hook in skipped sc.

Repeat from * across, making last half of joint puff st in last sc, make a dc in last sc. Ch 1, turn.

3rd row: Sc in first st, 2 sc in each joint puff st across, sc in top of turning chain. Ch 3, turn. Repeat 2nd and 3rd rows alternately until piece measures 34 inches.

March 18 Beautiful Bath Mat

Materials

100% cotton yarn

No. 2 Steel Crochet Hook

Starting at bottom, ch 132 to measure 22 inches.

1st row: Sc in 2nd ch from hook, * holding back on hook the last loop of each tr, make 3 tr in next ch, thread over and draw through all loops on hook (cluster made), sc in next 3 ch.

Repeat from * across, ending with sc in last ch. Ch 1, turn.

2nd row: Sc in each st across. Ch 1, turn. 3rd row: * Sc in next 3 sc, make a cluster in next sc.

Repeat from * across. Ch 1, turn. 4th row: Repeat 2nd row. Ch 1, turn. 5th row: Sc in first sc, * make a cluster in next sc, sc in next 3 sc.

Repeat from * across, ending with sc. Ch 1, turn.

Repeat 2nd to 5th rows incl until piece measures 34 inches, ending with the 5th row. Break off.

March 19 Curtain Bracelet

Materials

Worsted weight yarn (2 colors, A & B)

No. 4.5 Hook

Button

Instructions

Start with A, 24 ch

1. sc in ea ch; 1 ch, turn

2. *sc in next st, ch, (dc in next st) 3 times, sk 2 st* Repeat * to * along row; 1 ch, turn.

3.*sc in next st, ch, 3 dc in next ch sp* Repeat * to * along row ending with a sc in last st; 1 ch, turn.

4..*sc in next st, ch, 3 dc in next ch sp* Repeat * to * along row ending with a sc in last st; 1 ch, turn.

5.*sc in next st, ch, 3 dc in next ch sp* Repeat * to * along row; ending with (sc, ch, 3 dc) in last sc (=increment); 1 ch, turn.

6-9.Like Row 3

10.sc in ea sc. Cut A.

Join B in a corner at beginning of the left short sides;

1. 1 ch, sc all around, distributing uniformely scs on short-est sides, and making 3 sc in corners st; join with sl st in first sc. Now work only on the left short side you joined B in:

2. sc on ea sc of the side;1 ch, turn;

3.sc on ea dc on first half of the side, 4 ch, sc on ea rem sc. 1 ch, turn

4.sc on ea sc, sc in ea ch of the 4-ch loop (the buttonhole). Cut thread, weave in ends

Sew a button at the middle of the right short side , corresponding to buttonhole

March 20: Wreath curtain pull

Materials

Pearl cotton size 5

Steel crochet No. 7

Medium wire, 6 inches

Instructions

With Green ch 3, s c in 2nd st from hook, sl st in next st of ch, ch 3 to turn all rows.

2nd Row—Sl st in 3rd st from hook, sl st in next sl st, s c in next s c.

3rd Row—Sl st in 3rd st from hook, s c in next s c, sl st in next sl st. Repeat the last 2 rows until strip measures about 4½ inches, cut thread leaving a length. Sew the 2 ends together.

With Red embroider 4 groups of 3 French knots at intervals.

BOW—With Red ch 50, cut thread. Tie a bow and sew in position as illustrated.

Cut wire to size of wreath and overcast to wrong side. With Green crochet a ch about 10 inches long. Double in half and sew to top of wreath.

March 21: Curtain tie back pattern

Materials

Skein main color and contrasting color (A & B)

Crochet hook size 0

Instructions

Make 10 leaves as follows

With A ch 8, join (with slip st) to form ring, ch 1, [3 sc, 3 hdc, 3 dc, 3 tr (yo twice), 3 dc, 3 hdc, 3 sc] all in ring, join in first sc, fasten off. Flower

With B make a loop on hook, ch 2, 8 sc in 2nd ch from hook, join in first sc.

Rnd 2 - Ch 1, [1 sc and ch 1] all in joined st and each remaining st, join in first sc; (8 sps in rnd).

Rnd 3 - [1 slip st, ch 3, 1 tr, 2 long tr (yo 3 times), 1 tr, ch 3, 1 slip stl all in first sp and each remaining sp around, join in first slip st, fasten off.

Make 2 Rings

With B ch 8, join to form ring. Work a slip st in each ch around, join in first slip st, fasten off.

March 22: Crocheted Towel Topper

Materials

Kitchen towel

Ticket hole punch

Crochet hook 4 mm

Worsted weight yarn

Instructions

Row 1: Join yarn on the 1st hole, ch 1, esc (see esc tutorial below) in each hole across, turn.

Row 2: Ch 4 (counts as 1st tr), (tr tog the next two sts) across, tr on the last st, turn. (see tr tog tutorial below)

Row 3: Repeat row 2.

Row 4: Ch 3 (counts as dc), dc in each st across, turn.

Row 5: Repeat row 4, turn.

Row 6: Ch 4 (counts as tr), (tr tog next 2 sts) twice, ch 1, skip 1 st, (tr tog next 2 sts) twice, tr on last st., turn.

Row 7: Ch 1, sc in each st, turn.

Row 8: Ch 1, (sc tog next 2 sts) 3 times, sc on last st, turn.

Row 9: Ch 1, (sc tog next 2 sts) twice, sl st on last st. Fasten off and weave in ends.

March 23: Lazy Wave Hand Towel

Materials

Crochet hook 5mm

Worsted weight cotton yarn (your choice of color)

Instructions

Row 1: dc in 4th ch from hook, dc in next 3 ch, [dc decrease, dc decrease, 1 dc in next 3 ch, 2dc in next 2 ch, 1 dc in next 3 chs] 3 times, dc decrease, dc decrease, 1 dc in next 2 ch, 2dc in last ch, ch 3, turn (45).

Row 2: dc in next 3 dc, [dc decrease, dc decrease, 1 dc in next 3 dc, 2dc in next 2 dc, 1 dc in next 3 dc] 3 times, dc decrease, dc decrease, 1 dc in next 2 dc, 2dc in last dc, ch 3, turn (45).

Rows 3-41: dc in next 3 dc, [dc decrease, dc decrease, 1 dc in next 3 dc, 2dc in next 2 dc, 1 dc in next 3 dc] 3 times, dc decrease, dc decrease, 1 dc in next 2 dc, 2dc in the 3rd ch of the ch 3 you made at the end of the previous row, ch 3, turn (45).

Finish off and weave in ends.

March 24: Hand Warmers

Materials

5-oz worsted yarn

5.5 mm crochet hook

Tapestry needle

Instructions

Crochet a 3.5-inch long chain

R1: Skip one chain; 1 double crochet in each stitch; chain 1; turn

R2: repeat R1 to the length you desire

Tie off, allowing a long tail for stitching

Fold the piece into half along the length

Use the tapestry needle to stitch along the side; leave space for a thumb hole

Tie off and weave through with yarn

Turn it inside out to leave seam inside.

March 25 Dish Towel

Materials

Worsted cotton yarn

Hook size I

Instructions

R1: Ch42. Insert hook in 2nd ch from hook, yo and pull up a lp. (2 loops on hook)

Insert hook in next ch, yo and pull up a loop. (3 loops on hook)

Sk next ch.

Insert hook in next ch, yo and pull up a loop. (4 loops on hook)

(Yo, draw through 2 loops) three times.

Work 1 ltr in ea rem ch. (38 sts)

R2: Ch4, turn. Ltr in ea st across. (38 sts)

Rs 3-24: Rep R2.

Border

R1: Ch1, turn. Sc evenly around the entire pattern, placing 3sc in ea corner.

Rs2-4: Ch1, turn. Sc in ea st around, placing 3sc in ea corner.

Join with sl st in first sc made on R4.

Fasten off.

March 26: One Skein Tunisian Scarf

Materials

Homespun yarn

9 mm afghan hook

Instructions

Ch 15

Row 1: with one loop on, tss across the chain, return row

Row 2: ch 2 (counts as first tdc), tdc across the row, return row

Row 3 - : repeat Rows 1 and 2, until you reach the desired length, or until you reach the end of the skein.

Bind off using sc.

March 27: Royal Splendor Afghan

Materials

Afghan hook No. 6

White embroidery (6 balls)

56 balls blue embroidery

Instructions

Strip (Make 5)

Starting at narrow end with Blue, ch 45 to measure 9 1/4 inches. Work in afghan stitch - 45 loops on hook - until piece measures 62 inches. Sew Strips neatly together on wrong side.

Edging

1st rnd: Attach Blue and work sc closely together around all sides, making 3 sc in each corner and keeping work flat. Join. Drop Blue.

2nd rnd: Attach White and make an sc in back loop of each sc around, making 3 sc in center sc of each corner. Join and break off.

3rd rnd: Pick up Blue, sc in each sc around, making 3 sc in corner sc.

March 28: Afghan Stitch Coaster

Materials

Afghan hook size G

Worsted weight yarn

Instructions

R1: With Soft White, ch14, draw up a lp in the 2nd ch from hook. Draw up a loop in ea rem ch.

Yo, draw through the one lp. (Yarn over and draw through 2 lps) across.

Rs2-12: Draw up a lp in each vertical bar (14 lps on hook)

Yo, draw through one lp. (Yarn over and draw through 2 lps) across.

Do not fasten off.

Border:

R1: With Soft White, Ch1, sc evenly around entire coaster placing (sc, ch1, sc) in each corner stitch.

Fasten Off.

R2: Join Hunter Green in any stitch. Sc in same spaces where you placed the singles on R1, working over those singles as you go. Sc in ea sc. 3 sc in ea corner.

Fasten Off.

March 29: Bridal hankie

Materials

Desired length of ribbon

No. 10 cotton

Hook size 7

Instructions

Row 1: Ch 51, Sc in 2nd ch from hook and in each ch across. Ch 1, turn.

Rows 2-63: Sc in each st across. Ch 1, turn.

Row 64: Sc in each st across.

Border: * Ch 3, Do Not Turn, sk next row or st, sc in end of next row or st. Rep from * around. Join with sl st in 1st sc on border. Sl st in next ch 3 sp.

Rnd 2: Ch 5, dc in same sp. (dc, ch 2, dc) in each rem ch 3 sp. Join with sl st in 3rd ch of beg ch 5.

Rnd 3: Sl st in next ch 2 sp. Ch 5, dc in same sp. (dc, ch2, dc) in each ch 2 sp around. Join with sl st in 3rd ch of beg ch 5.

Fasten Off

Finishing: Add ribbon by weaving it in and out of Rnd 1 of the border. Tie a bow in the corner.

March 30: Bridal Garter

Materials

Ribbon of desired length

Size 7 steel hook

Cotton No. 10

Instructions

Row 1: Ch 135, join with sl st to form a ring. Ch 5. * Sk next ch, tr in next ch, ch 1. Rep from * around. Join with sl st in 4th ch of beg ch 5.

Edging:

Ch 3, (dc, 4ch picot,2dc) in same sp. Sc in next tr. * (2dc, 4-ch picot, 2 dc) in next tr. Sc in next tr. Rep from * around. Join with sl st in top of beg ch 3.

Fasten Off

Join thread with sl st in the foundation ch at the base of any tr st. Ch 3, (dc, 4-ch picot, 2dc) in same sp. Sc in next tr. *

(2dc, 4-ch picot, 2dc) in next tr. Sc in next tr. Rep from * around. Join with sl st in top of beg ch 3.

Fasten off.

Weave ribbon through center and tie a bow.

March 31 Cotton Wreath Tube Chain

Materials

One skein for each color you want

Size F crochet hook

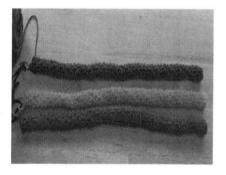

Instructions

Chain 2

5 sc in 2nd ch from hook. Mark first stitch for beginning of round and move marker up for each round.

sc in each sc around for 55 rounds.

Sl st

Cut yarn leaving a long tail. Knot yarn by pulling the yarn tail through the loop of yarn that is on the hook. The long yarn tail will be used later for sewing one end of the tube to the other.

April
April 1. Roanoke Dishcloth

Start this dishcloth with 45 chains

Row 1

Start with a double crochet in the fourth chain from the hook

Double crochet in the following chain then skip three chains (2 DC, CH 2, 2 DC).

In the next chain, skip three chains again, then DC in the next 3 chains and repeat this across, then turn over.

Row 2

Start with three chains, which will count as double crochet, then DC in the next 2 DC (2 DC, CH 2, 2 DC) in the next chain.

2 spaces, skip 2 DC, DC and 2 DC in the next three DC across the chain and turn

Repeat the second row until your pattern is around 10 inches, but do not turn.

Add another round of single crochet around the 4 edges then fasten.

To finish it up, weave in the ends.

April 2 The Dandelion Dishcloth

First Row

From the right side, 2 DC in the fourth chain from the hook

Skip 2 chains, DC in each of the following 5 chains; skip 2 chains (2 DC, chain 1, 2 DC).

In the following chain repeat the following two times; skip 2 chains, DC in each of the following 5 chains; skip 2 chains (2 DC, chain 1, 2 DC).

Make 3 double crochets in the next chain, then turn to the second row.

Second Row

Make three chains (which will count as double crochets). Follow this with 2 DC in the first DC.

*Make three chains, skip 4 double crochets, single crochet in the next double crochet, 3 chains.

Repeat two times the instruction from *

Make 3 chains, skip 4 double crochets, single crochet in the next DC

Make three chains, 3 DC in the third chain of the beginning chain 3, then turn.

Third Row

CH 3. Skip the first DC then DC in the next two DC

Repeat this two times then turn

Fourth Row

Chain 1, single crochet in the first DC.

* Chain 3, 2 DC, CH 1, 2 DC in the first chain

Leave a space, chain 3, skip 4 double crochets, single crochet in the next DC

Repeat three times from * then turn

Fifth Row

Chain 3, 2 double crochets in the first single crochet.

* DC in the next 2 DC, DC in Chain 1 then leave a space

DC in the following 2 DC

Repeat from * two times

DC in another 2 DC, DC in the first chain, then leave a space

DC in the next 2 DC, 3 DC in the final SC then turn

Repeat three times, row 2 – 5

Repeat once, row 2 – 3

After the last row, do not turn

Work the first round of SC around all the 4 edges evenly, then fasten off and weave in the ends.

April 3 Beginners 2 Strand Crochet Afghan Pattern

Materials

48 ounces worsted weight yarn

Size P hook

Instructions

Row 1: Ch 79, sc in second ch from hook and each ch across (78 sc)

Row 2: Ch 3 turn, skip first sc, dc in each sc across.

Row 3: Ch 1 turn, sc in each dc across, sc in top of ch 3.

Rep rows 2 and 3 until desired length.

April 4 Basketweave Crochet Afghan Pattern

Materials

One Pound; 2 skeins Azure (Color A)

2 skeins Off White (Color B)

2 skeins Taupe (Color C)

2 skeins Country Basket Ombre (Color D).

Needles: Size I crochet hook.

Instructions

With Color A, ch 192.

Row 1: Sc in 3rd ch from hook and in next 27 chs, * change to Color B, sc in next 27 chs, change to Color A, sc in next 27 chs, repeat from *, end sc in last ch, ch 2, turn.

Row 2: Skip first sc, * working in front, dc around post of each of next 3 sc (FPDC), working in back, dc around post of each of next 3 sc (BPDC), repeat from * across picking up new colors where left off; end hdc in turning ch, ch 2, turn.

Row 3: Skip first st, * FPDC around FPDC, BPDC around BPDC, repeat from * across, picking up new colors where left off, end hdc in turning ch, ch 2, turn.

Row 4: Skip first st, * FPDC around BPDC, BPDC around FPDC, repeat from * across, picking up new colors where left off; end hdc in turning ch, ch 2, turn.

Row 5: Repeat Row 3.

Rows 6 - 21: Repeat Rows 2 - 5, fastening off each color on Row 21, turn.

Row 22: (Cable Row) Join Color D with sl st in first st, sc in same st, * ch 3, sk 2 st, sc in next st, turn. Sc in each ch of ch 3, sl st in next st, turn. Working behind ch 3, sc in skipped sts, repeat from *, end sc in turning ch, turn.

Row 23: Join Color B with sl st in first st, ch 2, [* 2 sc in next st, sc in next st, repeat from * until there are 27 sc (do not count beg ch 2), join Color C, ** 2 sc in next st, sc in next st, repeat from ** until there are 27 sc], join Color B, repeat from [to] across, end sc in last st, ch 2, turn.

Rows 24 - 43: Repeat rows 2 - 21.

Row 44: Repeat row 22.

Rows 45 - 175: Repeat rows 23 - 44 six times, omitting row 44 at end of row 175 and alternating colors as indicated by rows 1 - 44.

Add fringe of your choice.

April 5 Diamond Duo Scarf

Materials

Purple, lavender and off white yarn

Using Hook Size J

Instructions

With purple yarn chain 11

SC in 2nd ch from hook and across, 10 sc, ch1, turn

SC in stitch under ch1 and across, 10 sc, ch1, turn

Continue for 8 more rows, a total of 10 rows, on last row do not turn but ch 11

Repeat rows 2 through 4, until you have 14 "diamonds" made

Repeat with lavender yarn.

Put diamond rows together with off white. When joining the rows together, slip stitch in the back loop of the stitch closest to you and the front loop of the row being joined.

Join off white at bottom "point" of first diamond, sc around entire piece with two single crochets at every point, join.

CH2, double crochet in same stitch as joining, DC around with skipping one sc at narrowest part and 2DC at the point, join.

CH3, skip one dc, sc in next stitch, continue around, join and finish off.

Using up your stash and making many diamond rows would make a lovely blanket!

April 6 DC Keyhole Neck Scarf

Materials:

4ozs of any 4-ply Soft or Sport yarn

'I' hook   Yarn Needle

Instructions

Note: Ch2, does not count as a dc

Row 1: Ch 122, dc in the 3rd ch from the hook, and in each ch across, turn (120 dc)

Rows 2-6: Ch2, dc across, turn

Row 7: Ch2, dc across the next 86dc, ch13, skip 13dc, dc across remaining dc, turn

Row 8: Ch2, dc across each dc and ch, turn

Rows 9-12: Ch2, dc across, turn

Keyhole Edging:

With right side facing, join yarn to 1st dc of opening, sc around, join end off

Outer Edging:

Row 1: With right side facing, working along all sides, sc around, working 3sc at each corner, join

Row 2: For Women, (sc in the next st, sl st in the next st) around, join, end off

Row 2: For Men, rev sc around, join, end off

Weave ends

April 7 Diamond Stitch Neck Scarf

Materials:

7ozs of worsted weight yarn 'K' hook Yarn Needle Multiple of 4+2

Instructions

Row 1: Ch17 (23), sc in the 2nd ch from the hook and in each ch across 16 (22)

Row 2: Ch2, sc across

Row 3: Ch1, sc in the 1st sc, fptr around the 5th sc post in Row 1, (sc in the next 3sc, work Cluster in both the same sc as the last fptr, and, skipping 3sc, and in the next sc), 2 (3) times, fptr in the same sc of the last Cluster, sc in the last 2sc

Row 4: Repeat Row 2

Row 5: Ch1, sc in the next 3sc, Cluster in the fptr and in the next Cluster, sc in the 3sc, (Cluster, sc in the 3sc) 2(3) times, sc in the last 2sc

Row 6: Repeat Row 2

Row 7: Ch1, sc in the 1st sc, fptr around fptr, (sc in the next 3sc, Cluster) 2 (3) times, sc in the next 3sc, fptr in the last Cluster, sc in the last 2sc

 Repeat Rows 4-7 until scarf measures 36", ending with Row 7

Ch1, sc around the sides and bottom and top of scarf, join, end off

April 8 draft dodger scarf

Materials

Size H/8/5mm Crochet Hook, 3½ oz.

yarn needle.

Instructions

Rnd. 1: ch17, sc in 2nd ch from hook, dc in next ch, *sc in next ch, dc in next ch*, repeat from *to* 6 times, ch1, turn.   16st

Rnd. 2: sc in first dc, dc in next sc, *sc in next dc, dc in next sc*, repeat from *to* 6 times, ch1 turn.   16st

Repeat rnd. 2 until scarf is desired length, fasten off on final rnd, weave in ends.

April 9 Earthen Lace scarf

Materials

I Hook

Lion Brand Jiffy solids

(A) 3 oz Taupe

(B) 3 oz Fisherman

Instructions

Ch 182

Row 1:

Using color A

Ch 183, 1 Hdc into 3rd ch from hook, 1 Hdc in each remaining chain. Fasten off color A

Row 2:

Join color B

Ch 3, 2 dc into first Hdc, *ch 2, skip next 3 Hdc, sc in next st, ch 5, sk 3 Hdc, sc in next st, ch 2, sk next 3 Hdc, 5 dc in next st, repeat from * ending with 3 dc in ch 3 of beg ch.

Row 3:

Ch 4, sk first dc, dc in next dc, ch 1, dc in dc, *ch 2, sk next ch 2 sp, sc in next ch 5 sp, ch 2, (dc, ch 1 in each of the next dc) four times, dc in next dc, repeat from * to the last 3 dc's, (dc, ch 1) twice, dc in 3rd ch of beg ch.

Row 4:

Ch 5, sk first dc, dc in next dc, ch 2, dc in next dc, *sk next sc, (dc, ch 2, in each of the dc) four times, dc in last dc, repeat from * to last sc, sk oast sc, (dc, ch 2) twice, dc in 3rd ch of beg ch. Fasten off color B

Row 5:

Join color A

Ch 2, 2 Hdc in each ch 2 sp and Hdc in each dc all the way across.

April 10 Easy and Warm 2 Stitch Scarf

Materials

3 Skeins of Jeager 100%

Size P (9 mm) hook

Instructions

-Ch 15 with color 1 (Beige or skien one)

-Double crochet in 4th chain from hook and dc in each chain across (12 DC) ch 3 and turn

-Repeat with 12 dc in each row for 20 in or until you run out of yarn

-Work in color 2 on last dc of last row ch 1 and turn

-Single crochet in each dc across (12 sc)

-Repeat for 20 in or until you run out of yarn

-Work the second skein of color 1 on last sc of last row ch 3 and turn

-Double crochet in each sc across (12 dc)

-Repeat for 20 in or until you run out of yarn (it should be the same length as section 1

-On last row use sc instead of dc.

-Weave in ends

April 11 Simple Crochet Scarf

Materials

Crochet Hook size K

Tapestry Needle

Stitch Marker

Worsted weight yarn

Instructions:

Ch 15.

Row 1: Place a marker in the first ch from your hook. sc in 3rd ch from hook. [ch 1, skip next ch, sc in next ch.] Rep sequence in brackets 5 more times across the row. Ch 1, turn.

Row 2: [sc in the next ch-1 sp, ch 1.] Rep the sequence in brackets 5 more times across the row. At the end of the row, work a sc st into the st where you placed the marker; you can remove the marker before working the stitch. Ch 1, turn.

Rows 3 and Up: The rest of the rows are all exactly the same as row 2, with one minor difference: at the end of the row you'll work your last sc st into the turning chain of the previous row. Rep this row until the scarf is as long as you want it to be.

Finish

April 12 Flower Scarf

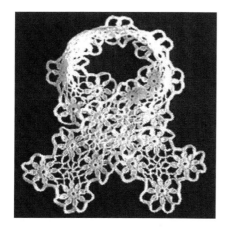

Materials:

100g ball white 8ply synthetic yarn, 5.00mm crochet hook.

Instructions

Begin by working 6ch, join with ss in 1st of 6ch to form a ring.

1st Round: Work 3ch, 15tr into ring, ss into 3rd ch.

2nd Round: Work 4ch, 2dtr into join, leaving last loop of each dtr on hook, yoh, pull through all sts [cluster made], * 10ch, miss next st, 3dtr cluster in next tr. Repeat from * finishing with 10ch, ss into top of 1st cluster.

Work next flower motif as above to *, 5ch, dc into 10ch loop on 1st motif, 5ch, miss next tr, 3dtr cluster in next tr, 5ch, dc into next 10ch loop on first motif, 5ch. Finish as 1st motif.

Join 3rd motif to next 2 10ch loops on 1st motif.

Join 4th motif to 3rd motif and 2nd motif, so that pattern forms 2 parallel lines of motifs.

Continue in this manner until you have joined 26 motifs. Do not fasten off.

Work edging as follows – Work 8dc into 10ch loops, 1dc into top of clusters, 4dc into 5ch sps. Fasten off.

Fill in Lace

Working from back of lace scarf, work 1dtr into each joining loop, ss in top of 1st dtr. Fasten off.

April 13 Frosty Scarf

Materials:

Yarn 100% acrylic, 355 yds/198

M hook

N hook

yarn needle

Instructions

Seed Spike stitch (sdsp): in seed stitch pattern, dc into ch-1 sp two rows below,

overlapping sc immediately.

With M hook, ch 252 LOOSELY. Switch to N hook.

Row 1: Sc into second ch from hook; sc into remaining ch; 251 sc.

Row 2: Ch 1 (count as 1st sc now & throughout), sc in next 2 sc, * ch 1, sk next sc, sc into next sc*, repeat from * to * until 2 sc remain, sc into each of last 2 sc. (123 ch-1 sp).

Row 3: Ch 1, sc in next sc, *ch 1, sk next sc, sc into next ch-1 sp*, repeat from * to * until 3 sc remain, ch 1, sk next sc, sc into each of last 2 sc.

Row 4: Ch 1, sc into each of next 2 sc, *dc into Row 2 ch-1 sp (sdsp made), sc into next ch-1 sp*, repeat from * to * until 2 sc remain, sc into each of next 2 sc.

Rows 5-13: Repeat Rows 2-4 three times.

Row 14: With M hook, sc in each st across. Fasten off.

April 14 Gina's Crochet Basket weave

Materials

Crochet hook J-10

100% acrylic yarn

Instructions

Ch 21

Row 1: dc 19, turn

Row 2: ch 2 *dc through front post, dc through back post, repeat from * to end of row, turn

Row 3: ch 2 *dc through back post, dc through front post, repeat from * to end of row

Repeat rows 2 – 3 to end.

Bind off and weave in ends.

April 15 Crochet Dish Cloth

Materials

50-gram cotton yarn

Crochet hook 8-5mm

Instructions

Crochet 35 stitch chains

Row 1: SC the 3rd CH from the hook; *CH1, SK 1 ST, 1 SC.

Repeat from * to the end of the row

CH1; Turn

Row 2: 1 Single ST in the first SC, CH1* SK 1 ST

Repeat from * to the end of the row

CH1; Turn

Repeat Row 1 & 2 until the cloth is square; Weave off the ends

April 16 Easy Baby Blanket

Materials

5-ounce baby yarn for the main color (4)

5-ounce baby yarn for the edges (1)

Crochet hook 5.5mm

Instructions

Crochet 65 stitch chain

Row 1: DC in the second chain ST from the hook; *CH 1, SK 1 ST; 1 DC in the next CH

Repeat from * to the end of the row; CH 1, Turn

Row 2: Follow the same procedure above until you have a square

Tie the ends and weave.

Edging

Use a slip stitch to attach the yarn at the corner; CH 2; 2 DC in the next ST

*CH 1, SK 1 ST, 3 DC in the next ST

Repeat from * round the blanket

Bind off and weave yarn

April 17 Baby Washcloth

Materials:

Mary Maxim Crochet Cotton - Mercerized Sportweight

Steel Hook - Size 1

Instructions

Round 1: With White, ch 40, sc in 2nd ch from hook and in each rem ch. Ch 3, turn. (39 sc)

Ch 3, turn. (note: turning chain 3 counts as the first hdc and ch 1.)

Round 2: Sk next st. Hdc in next st. *Ch 1, sk next st, hdc in next st. Rep from * across. Ch 1, turn.

Round 3: Sc in same st as beg ch-1. Sc in each ch-1 sp and in each hdc across. Ch 3, turn.

Round 4-33: Repeat Rows 2 & 3.

Round 34: Repeat Row 2.

Round 35: Sc in same st as beg ch-1. Sc in each ch-1 sp and in each hdc across. Ch 3. Do not turn.

April 18 Back Scrubber

Materials

Cotton Yarn (worsted weight 4ply)

Crochet hook H

Instructions

R1: Ch18, sc in 2nd ch from hook. Sc in ea rem ch. (17sc)

R2: Ch1, turn. Sc in same st. (4SC-PC in next st. Sc in next st.) across. (Eight 4SC-PC)

R3: Ch1, turn. Sc in ea st. (17sc)

R4: Ch1, turn. Sc in first 2sc. (4SC-PC in next st. Sc in next st.) across. (Seven 4SC-PC)

R5: Rep R3.

R6: Rep R2.

R7: Rep R3.

R8: Rep R4.

R9: Rep R3.

R10: Rep R2.

R11: Rep R3.

R12: Rep R4.

R13: Rep R3.

R14: Rep R2.

R15: Rep R3.

R16: Rep R4.

R17: Rep R3.

R18: Rep R2.

R19: Rep R3.

R20: Rep R4.

R21: Rep R3.

R22: Rep R2.

R23: Rep R3.

EDGE: Ch1, do not turn. Sc in ea st and in ea row end, placing 3sc in ea corner. Join with sl st.

Fasten Off

April 19 Mossy washcloth

Materials:

Size H Hook

A ball of cotton yarn:

Instructions

Ch 30

R1: sc in 2nd ch from hook, *sk1, ch1, sc* to end, turn.

R2: ch 2, sc in the first ch1 space, *sk sc, ch1, sc in ch1 space* to end, turn.

R3 onwards: Repeat R2 until your piece is square.

April 20 Spa cloth

Materials:

Worsted weight cotton yarn, Sugar & Cream about 1.25 ounces

H (5.0 mm) crochet hook

I (5.5 mm) crochet hook

Tapestry needle

Instructions:

With I hook ch 20.

Row 1: Sc in second chain from hook and in each chain across. Ch 1, turn. (19 sc)

Switch to H hook.

Row 2: Sc in first st. *Ch 3, sc in next st. Repeat from * across. Ch 1, turn. (18 loops)

Row 3: Keeping loops to the back side, sc in each sc across. Ch 1, turn. (19 sc)

Rows 4-23: Repeat rows 2 and 3.

Row 24: Sc in each sc across row.

Fasten off and weave in ends.

April 21 Scrubby Washcloth

Materials

Hook size: H

Yarn: Worsted weight cotton such as Peaches N Creme or Sugar N Cream

Instructions

Foundation row: Chain 40 loosely. You may want to use a hook one size larger for this chain only. Sc in 2nd chain from hook and in each ch across. Ch 1 and turn.

Row 1: This is the wrong side of the washcloth. Sc in first stitch. In next 37 stitches: sc, ch 3, insert hook in first chain above the sc, yo, and draw through both loops. Finish row with one sc. Ch 1 and turn.

Row 2: Sc across in each sc. Be sure to insert hook just to the right and below each nubble and fold nubble down toward you as you work the stitch. At the end of the row, make sure all nubbles are sticking out toward you. Ch 1 and turn.

Repeat rows 1 and 2 until the cloth is square. Finish off.

April 22 Towel Ring

Materials:

Hook size G/6-4.25mm

Crochet cotton (less than 1 oz.)

1 button (approx. ½ in.)

Instructions

Ring:

To begin, loop yarn around your hand twice to make a ring 2-2 ½ inches across. Using crochet hook, pull yarn through loop to make a slip stitch.

Ch 3 (counts as first dc). Dc around loop until you have about 50 dc. The number of stitches may vary depending on the size of your ring. Evenly space your dc to cover the yarn loop without letting the ring become "wavy" in appearance. Join with sl st to first dc. Turn.

Tab:

Ch 3 (counts as first dc), dc in next 9 stitches (10 dc total). Turn. Repeat for 10 rows.

Edging:

Ch 1, sc across last row. Make 2 more sc in last dc. Continue sc, spacing evenly, along side of tab. For ring, sc 3, sk 1 around to second side of tab. Sc evenly along second side. Make 2 sc in last stitch. Join and fasten off.

April 23 Placemat Set

Materials

Recycled grey cotton

4mm hook.

Instructions

row 1. Chain 50

row 2. chain 3, turn, tr in 3rd chain from hook, *skip one stitch, dc and then tr both into the next stitch*

* repeat to the end of the row and just 1dc in the last stitch of the row.

row 3. chain 2, turn, tr into the dc at the end of the last row (the 3rd chain/stitch from the hook), *skip one stitch, dc then tr both into the next stitch*

* repeat to the end of the row ending with 1 dc in last stitch of the row.

Repeat row 3 until the piece is as big as you would like the placemat – I completed 30 rows in total.

Do not fasten off but turn the work 90 degrees and continue in the direction you are going – dc all around the edge with 3dc in each corner. Fasten off and weave in ends.

April 24 Sunrise Placemat

Materials

Two colors of yarn

5mm Crochet hook

Tapestry Needle

Instructions

R1 – SC

R2 – R24 special stitch

R25 – SC

Change color for edging

Attach new color and sc crochet around placemat. Continue around with a slip stitch. You may choose on R25 to continue around your placemat with a sc stitch. I only did one row and fastened off. If you have trouble sc into the sides it may be better for you to single crochet around before doing the edging.

April 25 Sunrise Coaster

Materials

Two colors of yarn

5mm Crochet hook

Tapestry Needle

Instructions

R1 – SC

R2-R10 – special stitch

R11 – SC. Fasten off

Add Edging as with Placemat

If you do the same here are the finished measurements.

April 26 Pineapple Runner

Materials:

6 balls of White Yarn

Steel Crochet Hook No. 10.

Instructions

1st rnd: Attach thread to first ch-7 loop on side of a corner motif, ch 4, tr in same loop, * ch 5, 2 tr in next loop.

Repeat from * around, making 2 tr, ch 5 and 2 tr in each corner loop and ending with ch 5, sl st in top of starting chain. 2nd rnd: Sl st in next loop, ch 4, make 2-tr cluster in same loop, * (ch 5, make a 3-tr cluster in same loop) 2 more times; (ch 5, sc in next loop) twice; ch 5, make 3-tr cluster in next loop.

Repeat from * around. Join. 3rd rnd: Sl st in next 2 ch, sl st in loop, * ch 5, sc in next loop. Repeat from * around. Join and break off.

April 27 Coral Reef Motif

Materials

3 balls of White Yarn

Steel Crochet Hook No. 10.

1¾ yards of coral linen

Instructions

Starting at narrow end, ch 53 to measure 3¼ inches.

1st row: Tr in 13th ch from hook, * ch 5, skip 4 ch, tr in next ch. Repeat from * across (9 sps). Ch 6, turn.

2nd row: Holding back on hook the last loop of each tr make tr in next tr, 7 tr in next sp, tr in next tr, thread over and draw through all loops on hook (cluster made), * ch 5, make a cluster as before making first tr in same place as last tr. Repeat from * across, ending with tr in 4th ch of turning chain (9 clusters). Ch 9, turn.

3rd row: Tr in loop between next 2 tr, * ch 5, tr in next loop. Repeat from * across (9 sps). Ch 6, turn. Repeat 2nd and 3rd rows alternately for length desired, ending with 3rd row. Break off. Cut a piece of linen 12½ x 18½ inches. Make a rolled hem around all edges. Place Strip on right hand side over the linen and sew in place.

April 28 Mid-sized Placemat

Materials

2 balls of cotton yarn

Steel Crochet Hook No. 2/0

A hairpin lace staple, 2 inches wide.

Instructions

Make a strip of hairpin lace, having 35 loops on each side of staple. Break off.

To Form Center: Keeping the twist in all loops, attach thread through first 7 loops, make a sl st in same place, * make a sl st through next 7 loops. Repeat from * around. Join to first st made. Break off. Sew ends of hairpin lace together at center.

Make another strip, having 70 loops on each side.

To Join Strips: Keeping the twist in all loops, insert hook in first free loop on First Strip, insert hook through first 2 corresponding loops on Second Strip, draw the 2 loops from Second Strip through the single loop on First Strip (a sl st and an inc made), * insert hook in next loop on First Strip, draw loop through both loops on hook, insert hook through next 2 loops on Second Strip, draw both loops through loop on hook (another inc made). Repeat from * around. Tack last loop on hook in place on wrong side. Make 3 more strips of hairpin lace, having 35 loops more than on each previous strip. Join as before, increasing in every other loop on Third Strip, every 3rd loop on Fourth Strip and every 4th loop on Fifth Strip. Block to measurements.

April 29 Kentucky Placemat

Materials:

2 Skeins All Purpose Yarn

Crochet Hook Size F or 4.

Instructions:

Using single thread ch 70, turn on second ch from hook, 69 sc on ch.

Row 2—Ch 1 to turn, sc in each sc to end of row.

Row 3—Ch 1 to turn, sc in each sc to end of row. Repeat for 47 more rows, making 50 rows in all. To finish make 1 row of sc all around, inc 3 sts at corners to turn. Work a sl st around, using only back loop of previous row. Fasten off.

April 30 Aqua Toilet Seat Cover

4 balls of cotton yarn

Crochet Hook No. 9.

Instructions

ch 22.

1st row: Sc in 2nd ch from hook and in each ch across. Ch 1, turn.

2nd row: 2 sc in first sc (1 sc increased), sc in each sc to within last sc, 2 sc in last sc (another sc increased). Ch 1, turn.

3rd row: Sc in each sc across. Ch 1, turn. Repeat the 2nd and 3rd rows alternately until piece measures 6 inches. Work without increasing for 3 more inches. Then dec 1 sc at both ends of each row until 15 sc remain—to dec 1 sc, work off 2 sc as 1 sc. Break off.

Now work as follows:

1st rnd: Attach yarn to first sc of first row of center section, 3 sc in same place, sc closely around, making 3 sc in last sc of first row (having an even number of sc). Join.

2nd rnd: Ch 1, * sc in next sc, tr in next sc.

Repeat from * around. Join.

3rd rnd: Ch 1, sc in each st around, making 3 sc in center sc of each 3-sc group. Join.

4th rnd: Ch 1, * tr in next sc, sc in next sc. Repeat from * around. Join.

5th rnd: Repeat 3rd rnd. 6th rnd: Repeat 2nd rnd. 7th rnd:

Repeat 3rd rnd. 8th rnd: * Ch 3, skip 2 sc, sc in next sc. Repeat from * around. Join and break off. Make a chain 54 inches long and draw through last rnd of loops.

May
May 1: 100 Yard Dash

Materials

Approx 100 yards / 90ish metres 8ply DK yarn

5mm crochet hook

tube /dowel

Instructions

Row 1: ch 182

Row 2: hdc in 3rd ch from hook, hdc across

Row 3: DO NOT CH, DO NOT TURN!! Draw up loop and slip over tube, insert hook into next stitch to the right, draw up a loop and slip it over the tube. Continue drawing up loops of yarn through each successive stitch across the work.

Row 4: Remove tube from loops (this is the fun bit!). Form a slip stitch around the top of the first 4 loops (we're working from left to right again now). Hdc x 4 in these loops.

Pick up the next 4 loops and hdc x 4 in these loops. Continue in this manner across the work. Turn.

Row 5: ch 1, sc across work. Turn.

Row 6: *sl st, (sc, ch) in next st, sc, sl st** .... repeat from * to ** across work.

Weave in ends and you're done!

May 2 Scarf

Materials

• 860-124 Lion Brand Vanna's Choice® Yarn: Toffee

1 Ball (A)

• 860-130 Lion Brand Vanna's Choice® Yarn: Honey

1 Ball (B)

• 860-135 Lion Brand Vanna's Choice® Yarn: Rust

1 Ball (C)

• Lion Brand Crochet Hook - Size Q-19

• Large-Eye Blunt Needles (Set of 6) Scarf

Instructions

With 1 strand each of A, B and C held together, chain 76.

Row 1: Work 2 half double crochet in 3rd chain from hook, *half double crochet in next 2 chains, half double crochet 3 together over next 3 chains, half double crochet in next 2 chains, work 3 half double crochet in

next chain; repeat from * across to last 8 chains, half double crochet in next 2 chains, half double crochet 3

together over next 3 chains, half double crochet in next 2 chains, work 2 half double crochet in last chain.

Row 2: Chain 2 (does not count as a stitch here and throughout), turn, work 2 half double crochet first

stitch, *half double crochet in next 2 stitches, half double crochet 3 together over next 3 stitches, half double

crochet in next 2 stitches, work 3 half double crochet in next stitch; repeat from * across to last 8 stitches,

half double crochet in next 2 stitches, half double crochet 3 together over next 3 stitches, half double crochet

in next 2 stitches, work 2 half double crochet in last stitch.

Repeat Row 2 until all the yarn has been used. Fasten off.

Finishing

Weave in ends.

May 3: Easy Soft Scarf

Materials

Size K Hook

2 colors yarn (7 oz yarn - 6 oz of main color, 1 oz of contrast)

Instructions

Ch 170

Row 1: Dc in 4th ch from hook and in every st across. Ch 3, turn.

Row 2-7: Dc in dc next to hook and in every dc across. Ch 3, turn. End off.

Finishing edge - optional: Add a new color at the corner and make 2 dc, ch 2, 2 dc in same st. Now dc in each st to corner (2 dc, ch 2, 2 dc), repeat until all the way around scarf. Add fringe if desired.

May 4: Shell Scarf

Materials

Hook size I

4 oz of 4 ply soft worsted weight yarn.

Instructions

Ch 27 (width)

Row 1: Dc in 3rd ch from the hook-counts as 1 dc, 2 dc in same ch, (skip 1 ch, sc in next ch, skip 1 ch, 3 dc in next ch [shell made]) across, 3 dc in last ch, ch 3 and turn.

Row 2: Skip 1st st and sc in next st ~ in the center dc of shell, *skip next st, 3 dc in next st, skip 1 st, sc in next st* repeat from * to * across to next to last st- sc in that, ch 3 and turn.

Row 3: Make 2 more dc in base of the ch 3, *skip next st, sc in next st, skip next st, 3 dc in next st* repeat from *to* across finishing with 3 dc, ch 3 and turn.

Repeat rows 2 and 3 until scarf is 60-65" long (approx. 7" wide), adding new colors as you use up your scraps.

May 5: Fake afghan stitch scarf

Materials

100 gram yarn ball

5.50 mm Hook

Instructions:

Chain 21[29] Scarf should be (5 1/2 [8] inches wide)

Adjust number of chains but keep an odd number.

Row 1: Sc in 2nd chain from hook, and in each chain across.

Chain 1, Turn. (20 stitches) 20[28] stitches.

Row 2: Sc (single crochet) in first stitch, sc in second stitch,

*Chain 1, skip 1 stitch, sc in next stitch.

Repeat from * to last 2 stitches.

Chain 1, skip next stitch, Sc in last stitch. Chain 1, Turn.

Row 3: Sc in first stitch, sc in space, Chain 1, skip next stitch,

*sc in next space, chain 1, skip next stitch. Repeat from * to last stitch.

Sc in last stitch. Chain 1, Turn.

Repeat Row 3 for length: 40 inches for toddler, 102 inches for adult.

Last row: Sc in each stitch and space across. Fasten Off. Weave in loose ends.

Fringe for adult scarf:

End scarf with wrong side facing.

Chain 1, turn.

Slip stitch in first sc, chain 21, slipstitch in 2nd chain from hook and each chain.

*Slip stitch in next stitch, chain 21, slip stitch in 2nd chain from hook and each chain.

Repeat from * across end of scarf. Slip stitch in last stitch.

Fasten off.

With right side of other end of scarf facing, join yarn in first stitch with a slip stitch.

Work fringe as above.

May 6: Adult Scarf

Materials

Your choice of yarn and appropriate hook.

Instructions

Sc2tog

Insert hook in first st, YO, pull a loop through, insert hook in next st,

YO, pull a loop through, YO, and pull loop through 3 loops on hook.

Sc2tog done.

Instructions:

The first and last stitch of every row is both loop sc,

all other stitches are in back loop only for entire scarf.

Row 1: Ch 2, 3 sc in 2nd ch frm hk. Ch 1, Turn.

Row 2: 2 sc in first st, sc in next st, 2 sc in last st, Ch 1, Turn.

Row 3: 2 sc in first st, sc in each st across with 2 sc in last st. Ch 1, Turn

Row 4: 2 sc in first st, sc in ea st across with 2 sc in last st. Ch 1,Turn.

Repeat row 4 until scarf is wide enough. (5 1/2 inches for child, 8 inches for adult)

Row 5: Sc2tog, sc in each st across with 2 sc in last st. Ch 1, Turn.

Row 6: 2 sc in first st, sc in each st across to last 2 sts. Sc2tog. Ch 1, Turn.

Repeat Rows 5 and 6 until scarf is long enough, ending with row 6.

Row 7: Sc2tog, sc in each remaining st to last 2 sts. Sc2tog. Ch 1, Turn.

Repeat Row 7 until three sts remain. Sc3tog. Fasten off.

May 7: Neck Cozy

Materials:

2 balls cotton yarn

Hooks: size 6.5 mm (K) and size 6 mm (J)

2 large buttons

Instructions

Set Up Row: SC in second chain from hook, *chain 1, skip 1 chain, 1 SC in next chain, repeat from * to end. Turn.

Pattern Row: Chain 1, skip first SC, *1 SC in chain-1 space, Chain 1, skip 1 SC, repeat from *, ending by making SC in chain 1, turn.

With double strand of yarn, and larger hook, chain 92. Change to smaller (J) hook and work Set-Up Row of pattern across chain.

Rows 2 & 3: Work Pattern Row across stitches.

Row 4: (buttonhole row) Work 4 stitches (ch 1, sc, ch 1, sc), chain 3, skip 3 stitches (these three skipped stitches are: sc, ch 1, sc) and continue in pattern to end of row.

Row 5: Work Pattern Row as established, but when you come to the chain 3 space of the previous row, work (sc, ch 1, sc) in that space.

Rows 6 - 9: Work Pattern Row as established

Row 10: Work Buttonhole Row as before

Row 11: Work Pattern Row as established, and when you come to chain 3 space of the previous row, work (sc, ch 1, sc) in that space.

Row 12: Work Pattern Row as established. End off, turn, and work a row of sc across the short end of the neck cozy.

May 8: 2 strand chunky cowl scarf

Materials

260 meters of chunky wool

12mm crochet hook

Tapestry needle

Instructions

Foundation Chain: Ch 50 loosely, Slst to first ch to form round.

Row 1: Ch 1, SC into second ch from hook, SC in the butt (behind of each chain to make nice edge) of each ch. Slst into first SC of round to join round. (50 SC total).

Row 2: Ch 2 (does not count as one HDC), HDC into each SC until end. Slst into first HDC to join round. (50 HDC total).

Rows 3-7: Ch 2 (does not count as one HDC), HDC into each stitch until end. Slst into first HDC to join round. (50 HDC total).

Row 8: Ch 2 (does not count as one HDC), *HDC 4 stitches, HDC2tog (DEC), repeat from * 8 times. HDC in final 2 stitches. Slst to join round. (42 HDC total)

Rows 9-10: Ch 2 (does not count as one HDC), HDC into each stitch until end. Slst into first HDC to join round. (42 HDC total).

Row 11: Ch 2 (does not count as one HDC), *HDC 8 stitches, HDC2tog (DEC), repeat from * 4 times. HDC in final 2 stitches. Slst to join round. (38 HDC total).

Row 12-14: Ch 2 (does not count as one HDC), HDC into each stitch until end. Slst into first HDC to join round. (38 HDC total).

Row 15: Ch 2 (does not count as one HDC), *HDC 8 stitches, HDC2tog (DEC), repeat from * 3 times. HDC in final 8 stitches. Slst to join round. (35 HDC total).

Row 16: Ch 1, SC into each HDC til end, Slst to join round. (35 SC total).

May 9: Rippling Peacock Scarf

Materials

Cotton yarn

12mm crochet hook

Tapestry needle

Instructions

Ch 245.

Row 1: (RS) Turn, sk 3 ch (counts as dc), dc3tog, dc in next 9 sts, 5 dc in next st, dc in next 9 sts, *dc5tog, dc in next 9 sts, 5 dc in next st, dc in next 9 sts; rep from * across to last 4 ch, dc3tog, dc in last st. (243 sts)

Row 2: Turn, ch 3 (counts as dc, here and throughout), dc3tog, dc in next 9 sts, 5 dc in next st, dc in next 9 sts, *dc5tog, dc in next 9 sts, 5 dc in next st, dc in next 9 sts; rep from * across to last 4 sts, dc3tog, dc in t-ch.

Row 3: Turn, ch 3, dc3tog, ch 1, sk 1 st, (dc in next st, ch 1, sk 1 st) 4 times, 5 dc in next st, ch 1 (sk 1 st, dc in next, ch 1) 4 times, *sk 1 st, dc5tog, ch 1, sk 1 st, (dc, ch 1, sk 1 st) 4 times, 5 dc in next st, ch 1, (sk 1 st, dc in next st, ch 1) 4 times; rep from * to last 5 sts, sk 1 st, dc3tog, dc in t-ch.

Row 4: Rep Row 2, treating both dc and ch-1 sp as sts.

Row 5: Turn, ch 3, dc3tog, ch 2, sk 1 st, (pop, ch 2, sk 1 st) 4 times, (pop, ch 3, pop, ch 2) in next st, (sk 1 st, pop, ch 2) 4 times, *sk 1 st, dc5tog, ch 2, sk 1, (pop, ch 2, sk 1 st) 4 times, (pop, ch 3, pop, ch 2) in next st, (sk 1 st, pop, ch 2) 4 times; rep from * across to last 5 sts, sk 1 st, dc3tog, dc in t-ch.

Row 6: Turn, ch 3, 2 dc in next 5 ch-2 sps, 5 dc in ch-3 sp, *2 dc in next 4 ch-2 sps, dc in next ch-2 sp, dc in next st, dc in next ch-2 sp, 2 dc in next 4 ch-2 sps, 5 dc in ch-3 sp; rep from * across to last 5 ch-2 sps, 2 dc in next 5 ch-2 sps, sk 1 st, dc in t-ch.

Rows 7-9: Rep Rows 3-5.

Row 10: Turn, ch 3, 2 dc in next 5 ch-2 sps, (2 dc, ch 2, 2 dc) in ch-3 sp, *2 dc in next 4 ch-2 sps, dc in next ch-2 sp, dc in next dc, dc in next ch-2 sp, 2 dc in next 4 ch-2 sps, (2 dc, ch 2, 2 dc) in ch-3 sp; rep from * across to last 5 ch-2 sps, 2 dc in next 5 ch-2 sps, sk 1 st, dc in t-ch. Fasten off.

Finishing

Weave in ends.

May 10: Faux fabric Circle scarf

Materials

Holiday Yarns Nylon

Skein (1) in Wolverine

US G-6/4 mm crochet hook

Yarn needle.

Instructions

Ch 40.

Row 1: Turn, sk 2, (counts as first hdc, here and throughout), *dc in next ch, hdc in next ch; rep from * across. (39 sts)

Row 2: Turn, ch 3 (counts as dc here and throughout), *hdcBL in next st, dcBL in next st; rep from * across.

Row 3: Turn, ch 2, *dcBL in next st, hdcBL in next st; rep from * across.

Rep Rows 2-3 60 times (or until scarf measures approximately 49" (124.5 cm) long. Do not fasten off.

Fold short ends together and match up sts on each side. Seam together short edges with sl st through each side. Fasten off. Turn right side out (so seam is inside).

Finishing

With yarn needle, weave in ends

May 11: Arch Mesh scarf

Materials

50 g ball of German yarn

G hook

Instruction

Start with a starting chain of a multiple of 4 stitches plus 3. (For example, 8 + 3 = starting chain of 11; 12 + 3 = starting chain of 15; etc)

Row 1: Chain 5 (counts as first dc and ch 2), sc in 6th chain from hook, ch 2, skip 1 ch, *dc in next ch, ch 2, skip 1 ch, sc in next ch, ch 2, skip 1 ch, repeat from *, end row with dc.

Row 2: Ch 1, turn, *sc in dc of previous row, ch 2, dc in sc of previous row, ch 2, repeat from *, end row with sc in third ch of the ch 5.

Row 3: Ch 5, turn, *sc in dc of previous row, ch 2, dc in sc of previous row, ch 2, repeat from *, end row with dc.

Repeat rows 2 and 3 until scarf is desired length. Weave in ends.

As always, let me know if you have any questions or problems with the pattern.

May 12: Ashlea scarf

Materials

Crochet size K

100% cotton yarn

Instruction

Chain 20.

Row 1: Make cluster into the 4th ch from the hook), **skip a ch, v stitch in the next ch, skip a chain, cluster into the next ch**, repeat from ** to **. You should end with a cluster in the last chain. Ch 3, turn

Row 2: Skip the first sc, make a cluster in the next st, (which is the dc of the cluster below),

v stitch into the v stitch below, cluster into the DC of the cluster below, repeat from ** to **, ending with a cluster in the last DC of the last cluster. Do not stitch into the ch 3 turning chain.

ch 3, turn.

Repeat row 2 until your scarf is as long as you want it to be.

May 13: Basic Crocheted Neck Warmer

Materials

Tools: US "K" crochet hook

Needle

Thread or extra yarn

1 3/8" to 1/2" shank button

Instructions

Chain 81

Row 1. Half double crochet (HDC) in the back bump of the 2nd chain from the hook and into the bump of each chain across. (80 stitches), chain 1, turn.

Rows 2-9. *HDC into each stitch across, ch. 1, turn* repeat for each row.

Row 10. HDC into each stitch across, finish off at last stitch. Weave in ends.

Sew on button, about 4-5 inches from one end of the neck warmer. Use any hole at the opposite end as a buttonhole. Buttons with shanks work much better than flat buttons.

This neck warmer is meant to be a little longer, and overlap like a scarf. It can also just be wrapped around and tucked in if you want, without the button at all.

May 14: Cozy Crocheted Scarf

Materials

Size H hook

2 oz 4 ply worsted weight yarn

Instructions

Ch 22

Row 1: Sc in 2nd ch from hook, and in each ch across. Ch 1 and turn.

Row 2 - 140: Sc in 2nd ch from hook, and in each ch across, ch 1 and turn. Final row, end off with 3" tail of yarn. Weave in tail.

May 15: Five Petal Crocheted Flower

Materials

Worsted yarn

Crochet hook size G

Instructions

chain 5 and join with sl st to first chain to form ring.

Round 1: Ch 2 (counts as 1 dc) and work 15 dc into the ring, sl st to beginning chain.

Round 2: *Ch 3, skip 2 dc, sl st into next dc: repeat from * 4 more times ending in last stitch in base of beginning chain. (You now have five chained loops.)

Round 3: In each Ch 3 space work 1sc, 3 dc, 1 sc: join with a sl st to first sc.

End yarn, leaving a tail for joining. Weave in all ends.

May 16: Crossed in the middle Scarf

Materials

J hook

Scrap yarn worsted weight acrylic

Instructions

Row 1: Ch 200, dc in 4th ch from the hook, dc in each st across. Turn.

Row 2: Ch 2, hdc in each st across. (In Back Loops Only) Turn.

Row 3: Ch 3, *Skip a st, dc in the next st. Cross the front of that dc and dc in the skipped st. Repeat from * across. End with a dc in the last st. Turn.

Row 4: Ch 2, hdc in each st across. Turn.

Row 5: Ch 3, dc in each st across. Fasten off and weave in ends.

May 17: Family Hat

Materials

Size I hook

4 Ply worsted weight yarn

Instructions

Kids 2-7 (ch 36), Age 8-10 (ch 42), Age 11-14 (ch 48), teen and adult (ch 56).

Row 1: Dc in 3rd ch from the hook and in each ch across. Ch 2. Turn.

Rows 2-(as many rows as you need for width of head): Dc in 2nd st from hook across to end of row - in Back loops only-- to form ridge. Ch 2. Turn.

On your final row for the width -don't ch 2 at the end, just end off, leaving 18" tail.

Sew sides together.

May 18: Bling Bling and Little flowers

Materials

Crochet.

1 ball Bling Bling

1 ball novelty yarn

Hook K

Instructions

Holding Bling Bling and a novelty yarn together, chain 10 very loosely.

Double crochet (dc) into second chain from the hook and in each one of the following 8. (9dc) Chain 1 and turn.

*DC 9, chain 1, turn.

Repeat this row in bold until almost out of Bling Bling. Secure Bling Bling and cut. Leave the novelty attached.

If you have novelty left, do a fringe on both ends as follows:

Switch to smaller hook

Do 2 dc into each of your 9 dc. (18 dc) Chain 1, turn.

*DC 18 (1 into each), chain1, turn.

Repeat the row in bold intil fringe is 3". Repeat the fringe on the other end.

May 19: Flirty Kristen

Materials

Red Heart worsted weight yarn, Coral

Crochet hook size H

Scissors

Blunt or yarn needle

Instructions

ch 82.

Row 1- 1 hdc in third ch from hook and in each ch across. (81 hdc) Ch 1, turn.

Row 2- 1 sc in first hdc, 1 tr in next hdc, *1 sc in next sc, 1 tr in next hdc, rep from * across till last 2 sts, 1 sc in each of last 2 sts. (81 sts) Ch 2, turn.

Row 3- 1 hdc in each st across. (81 hdc) Ch 1, turn (Counts as first hdc of next row, throughout).

Row2 4 to 7- Rep rows 2 and 3. (81 sts)

Row 8- 1 sc in each hdc across. (81 sc) Ch 2, turn.

Row 9- 1 hdc in each of next 11 sts, ch 12, skip 12 sts, 1 hdc in next st and in each st till end of row. (67 hdc + 12 ch) (Keyhole started) Ch 1, turn.

Row 10- 1 sc in each st and in each ch across. (81 sc) (Keyhole completed) Ch 2, turn.

Row 11- 1 hdc in each st across. (81 hdc)

Rows 12 to 14- Rep rows 2 and 3. (81 sts) Ch 2, turn.

Row 15- 1 hdc in each st across.

Fasten off, weave in tails.

May 20: Bubbles

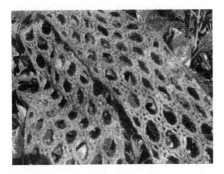

Materials

5mm Hook and 4.5mm Hook

Instructions

Use the 5mm hook to chain 27 after this use the 4.5mm

Row 1/ 1 dc into 2nd chain from hook, dc across to end, turn

Row 2/ 1ch, 1 dc into each of first 2 dc *5ch, skip 2 dc, 1dc into each of next 3 dc* repeat with only 2 dc at end of row, turn

Row 3/ 1ch, 1dc into first dc * 5dc into next 5ch arch, skip 1dc, 1dc into next

dc* repeat to end, turn.

Row 4/ 5ch, skip first 2dc, 1dc into each of next 3dc * 5ch, skip 3dc,

1dc into each of next 3dc* repeat to last 2 stitches, 2ch, 1 treble into

last dc. turn

Row 5/ 1ch, 1dc into first treble, 2dc into 2ch space, skip 1dc, 1dc into next

dc, * 5dc into next 5ch arch, skip 1dc, 1dc into next dc* repeat to last 2ch

space. 2dc into last space, 1dc into 4th chain of previous row. turn

Row 6/ 1ch, 1dc into each of first 2dc, * 5ch, skip 3dc, 1dc into each of next 3dc*

repeat to end, ending with 2dc

Repeat rows 3-6 until desired length.

May 21: Bumpy Scarf pattern

Materials

Standard 4-ply worsted weight of 2 different colors

Size I hook

Instructions

Color A, ch 196

Row 1: *SC in second ch from hook, DC in next ch, TC in next ch*, repeat across row, ending with TC in last st, break off. Attach color B, ch 1, turn.

Row 2: SC in first st, DC in next stitch, TC in next st, repeating across row, ending with TC in turning ch, break off. (You will be doing a SC in the TC of the previous row, DC in the DC of previous row, and TC in SC of previous row). Attach color C, ch 1, turn.

Repeat row 2, alternating colors A, B, and C until you have 10 rows, ending with color A.

Weave in ends.

May 22: Arithmancy scarf

Materials:

3 skeins of Worsted Weight Yarn

H hook

Yarn needle

Instructions:

Chain 32

Row 1: With Blue HDC into each chain across, ch 2. Turn.

Row 2-3: HDC in each HDC across, ch2 turn.

Row 4: HDC in each HDC across. Finish off.

Row 5: Join Silver, chain four (serves as first TRC). TRC in each HDC across. Finish off.

Row 6: Join green. Chain 1. SC in each TRC across, chain 1. Turn

Row 7-8: SC in each SC across. Finish off.

Row 9: Join Blue. HDC in each SC across. Chain 2, turn.

Row 10-End: Repeat rows 2-9 until desired length is achieved. Finish off and weave in ends. Attach tassles if desired.

May 23: Brite Scarf

Materials:

Caron International's Simply Soft Brites

8 oz. Embroidery Print (Color A), 6 oz. Lemonade (Color B), 4 oz. Grape (Color C).

Size Q crochet hook

Instructions

With 2 strands held tog using color A, ch 110.

Row 1: Dc in 3rd ch from hook, * ch 2, sk 1 ch, dc in next 2 dc, * rep from * across row. Fasten off.

Row 2: Attach color B on top of last dc. Ch 5, * puff stitch in next ch-2 space, ch 2, * rep from * across. End dc in last dc. Fasten off.

Row 3: Attach color A, ch 3, dc in ch-2 space, * ch 2, 2 dc in next 2 ch space * rep from * across. End dc in 4th and

3rd ch of ch-5. Fasten off.

Row 4: Attach color C, rep Row 2.

Row 5: Rep Row 3.

Row 6: Rep Row 2, with color B.

Row 7: Rep Row 3.

Fasten off.

Fringe: Cut 14" strands of each color. Knot 3 strands in each st across both short ends of scarf. Trim fringe.

May 24: Brite Hat

Materials

Caron International's Simply Soft Brites

8 oz. Embroidery Print (Color A), 6 oz. Lemonade (Color B), 4 oz. Grape (Color C).

Hat size H crochet hook

Instructions

With color A, ch 4, join with sl st to form ring.

Rnd 1: Ch 3, work 9 dc in ring. Join with sl st to top of ch 3.

Rnd 2: Ch 3, dc at base of ch 3, work 2 dc in ea dc around (20 sts) counting ch 3 as one st. Join as before.

Rnd 3: Ch 3, * 2 dc in next dc, 1 dc in next dc, * rep from * around, work 2 dc in last dc, (30 sts). Join.

Rnd 4: Ch 3, * 2 dc in next dc, 1 dc in ea of next 2 dc, * rep from * around. Join.

Rnd 5: Continue to work in dc and inc 10 dc evenly spaced

around (working 1 more st bet inc). Fasten off.

Rnd 6: Attach color B, rep Rnd 5. Rnd 7: Ch 3, dc in ea dc around (60 dc). Join.

Rnd 8: Attach color A, rep Rnd 7. Fasten off.

Rnd 9: Attach color C, rep Rnd 7. Fasten off.

Rnd 10: Attach color A, rep Rnd 7. Fasten off.

Rnd 11: Attach color B, ch 5, * sk 2 dc, puff stitch in next st, ch 2, * rep from * around. End puff st in last st. Join to ch 3. Fasten off. Rnd 12: Attach color A, ch 3, dc in ch-2 sp, * ch 1, 2 dc in next ch-2 sp, * rep from * around. Join to ch 3. Rnds 13-14: Ch 1, sc in ea stitch around. Join. Fasten off.

May 25: Chained Fringe Scarf

Materials

Worsted Weight Yarn

Size J hook

Instructions

Chain to desired length (approximately 60 inches) then chain 40 more. Finish off

Start a new chain

Chain 20 then join with a slip stitch to the 20th chain of the first row. Sc in each stitch until the 20th chain from the end then chain 20 not connecting them to the first row. Finish off.

Chain 20 then join to first sc of second row. Sc in each sc. Chain 20 after last sc. Finish off.

Repeat this process until scarf is desired width.

May 26: Chakra scarf

Materials

US D-3 (3.25mm) hook

100% cotton yarn

Instructions

Chain 59.

Row 1 (RS): Dc in fourth ch from hook, dc in next ch (beg block made), dc in each remaining ch across (27 blocks made), turn—28 blocks.

Rows 2 and 3: Ch 3, dc in each st across, turn.

Row 4: Ch 3, dc in next 2 sts (beg block made), [ch 1, skip next st, dc in next st (mesh made)] 26 times, dc in last 2 sts (block made), turn—2 blocks and 26 mesh.

Row 5: Repeat Row 4.

Row 6: Repeat Row 2.

Row 7: Repeat Row 4.

Row 8: Work beg block, 6 mesh, 2 blocks, 7 mesh, 2 blocks, 9 mesh, 1 block, turn.

Row 9: Work beg block, 8 mesh, [4 blocks, 5 mesh] twice, 1 block, turn.

Row 10: Work beg block, 5 mesh, 5 blocks, 4 mesh, 5 blocks, 7 mesh, 1 block, turn.

Rows 11–84: Continue working blocks and mesh as shown in chart.

Repeat Rows 19–84 twice.

Repeat Row 4 three times.

Repeat Row 2 once.

Repeat Row 4 twice.

Repeat Row 2 three times. Fasten off.

Finish off

Using yarn needle, weave in all ends. Block lightly

May 27: Chevron Scarf

Materials:

Worsted weight yarn

Size H (5.00 mm) Hook

Yarn needle

Instructions

Ch 23

Row 1: Hdc in 3rd ch from hook, hdc in 8 ch, skip 2 ch, hdc in 10 ch. [20 hdc]

Row 2: Ch 2, hdc in blo of 8 sts, skip 2 sts, hdc in blo of 9 sts. [18 hdc]

Note: This is the right side.

Row 3: Ch 2, hdc in blo of 7 sts, skip 2, hdc in blo of 8 sts. [16 hdc]

Row 4: Ch 2, hdc in blo of 6 sts, skip 2, hdc in blo of 7 sts. [14 hdc]

Row 5: Ch 2, hdc in blo of 5 sts, skip 2, hdc in blo of 6 sts. [12 hdc]

Row 6: Ch 7, hdc in 3rd ch from hook, hdc in 4 chains, hdc in blo of 4 sts, skip 2 sts, hdc in blo of 5 sts. [15 hdc]

Row 7: Ch 7, hdc in 3rd ch from hook, hdc in 4 ch, hdc in blo of 3 sts, skip 2 sts, hdc in blo of 9 sts. [18 hdc]

Repeat rows 3-7, until scarf is 1/2 the desired length, ending with row 5.

Center row:

Ch 1, sc in blo of 2 hdc, hdc in blo across to last 2 sts, sc in blo only in last 2 sts. Fasten off.

On second strip don't fasten off. Put the two strips right sides together and slip stitch them together working in the blo. Weave in ends.

May 28: Claudia Scarf

Yarn: Approx 680m of 4ply

Hook: 3.00mm

Instructions

Chain 62 (or 54 for a narrower scarf).

Row 1: 1 dc into 6th ch from hook, *miss 2 ch, 5 dc into next ch, miss 2 ch, 1 dc into next ch, ch 1, miss 1 ch, 1 dc into next ch. Repeat from * until end.

Row 2: Ch 4 (counts as 1 dc plus 1 ch), miss ch sp, 1 dc into dc, *miss 2 dc, 5 dc into next dc (the 3rd dc of the shell), miss 2 dc, 1 dc into dc, ch 1, miss ch sp, 1 dc into dc. Repeat from * until end putting last dc into 4th of 5 ch.

Row 3: Ch 4 (counts as 1 dc plus 1 ch), miss ch sp, 1 dc into dc, *miss 2 dc, 5 dc into next dc (the 3rd dc of the shell), miss 2 dc, 1 dc into dc, ch 1, miss ch sp, 1 dc into dc. Repeat from * until end putting last dc into 3rd of 4 ch.

Row 4 – 85: Repeat row 3

When you have completed the first half of the scarf, fasten off then rejoin yarn into back of foundation chain. Make the second half of the scarf as you made the first half.

Block if desired.

May 29: Caitlin's V-Stitch Scarf

Materials:

G (4.0 mm) hook

100 g DK yarn, any color

Yarn needle (for weaving in ends)

Instructions

ch 28

Row 1: hdc in 3rd ch from hook and in each ch across; turn

Row 2: ch 2 (counts as first hdc), hdc in 2nd stitch from hook and in each st across; turn

Row 3: ch 3 (counts as dc), *sk 2 sts, dc-ch1-dc in next st*, repeat from * to * across, 1 dc in last st; turn

Row 4: repeat row 3

Row 5: repeat row 3

Row 6: repeat row 2

Row 7: repeat row 2

Row 8: repeat row 2

Alternate repeats of Row 3 (3 rows) and Row 2 (another 3 rows), until the scarf is as long as you want and/or you run out of yarn, making the last Row 2 repeat only 2 rows.

Fasten off, weave in ends.

May 30 Tablecloth Motif

Materials

100% White cotton yarn

Crochet Hook No. 6.

Instructions

Starting at center, ch 7. Join with sl st to form ring.

1st rnd: Ch 3, 2 dc in ring, (ch 6, 3 dc in ring) 5 times; ch 6. Join to top of ch-3.

2nd rnd: Ch 4, holding back on hook the last loop of each tr, make tr in next 2 dc, thread over and draw through all loops on hook (cluster made), * ch 5, in next loop make sc, ch 3 and sc; ch 5, make a cluster over next 3 dc.

Repeat from * around. Join and break off.

May 31: Square Pillow pattern

Materials

7 balls of yarn

Steel Crochet Hook No. 2/0

Instructions

Chain 16 inches long.

1st row: 2 dc in 4th ch from hook, * skip next 3 ch, in next ch make sc, ch 2 and 2 dc.

Repeat from * across until row measures 14 inches, ending with an sc. Cut off remaining chain. Ch 3, turn.

2nd row: 2 dc in first sc, * in next ch-2 sp make sc, ch 2 and 2 dc. Repeat from * across, ending with sc. Ch 3, turn. Repeat 2nd row until piece is square. Break off.

June

June 1: Father's Day Fold and Sew Wallet

Materials:

Fine Weight Yarn (approximately 50 yards)

Crochet Hook G (4.00 mm)

Instructions

Row 1: ch 31, sc in second ch from hook and each ch across: 30 sc

Rows 2-12: ch 1, turn, sc in each sc across: 30 sc

Row 13: turn, sl st in first 4 sc, sc in next 22 sc: 22 sc

Rows 14-24: ch 1, turn, sc in next 22 sc

Row 25: turn, sl st in first 3 sc, sc in next 16 sc: 16 sc

Rows 26-36: ch 1, turn, sc in next 16 sc

Finish off.

June 2: Spiral Coaster

Materials:

Medium Weight Yarn (approximately 15 yards of each color)

Crochet Hook H (5.0 mm)

Instructions

Round 1: With Color A, make an adjustable ring ch 1, 6 sc into ring: 6 sc

Round 2: With Color B, 2 sc in each sc around: 12 sc

Round 3: With Color A, (2 sc in next sc, sc in next sc) around: 18 sc

Round 4: With Color B, (2 sc in next sc, sc in next sc) around: 27 sc

Round 5: With Color A, (2 sc in next sc, sc in next sc) until 1 sc remains, 2 sc in last sc: 41 sc

Round 6: With Color B, (2 sc in next sc, sc in next 2 sc) until 2 sc remain, 2 sc in next sc, sl st in last sc: 55 sts

Finish off.

June 3: Gift Card Holder

Materials:

Medium Weight Yarn (approximately 20 yards of main color and 3 yards of contrasting color)

Crochet Hook G (4.00 mm)

Yarn Needle   crochet yarn size 4

Instructions

Gift Card Holder:

Round 1: with main color, ch 19, sl st in first ch to join and make a ring: 19 ch

Round 2: sc in each ch around, place marker: 18 sc

Round 3 – 13 sc in each sc around: 18 sc

Round 14: sl st into each sc around: 18 sl st

Finish off.

June 4 Business Card Holder

Materials:

Turquoise Medium Worsted Weight Yarn (approximately 50 yards)

Crochet Hook H (5 mm)

Sewing Needle

Sewing Thread

1 Buttons (1/2″ in diameter)

Crochet yarn size 4

Instructions

Row 1: Ch 14, sc in second ch from hook and in each sc across. 13 sc

Row 2-15: ch 2, sc in each sc across.

Finish off.

Finishing

Fold crocheted square in half and sl st both the left sides together and finish off. Then, sl st the right sides of the business card holder together. Finish off and weave in ends.

June 5 Business Card Sleeve

Materials:

Medium Weight Yarn (small amount of main color)

Yarn used in photo: Caron Simply Soft Yarn

Crochet Hook I (5.50 mm)   crochet yarn size 4

Instructions

Round 1: ch 15 (or a chain that is as long as the width of your cards), sc in second ch from hook and in each ch across, working into remain loops on opposite side of chain, sc in each ch across, place marker: 28 sc

Round 2 – 12: sc in each sc around: 28 sc

Finish off.

June 6 Extra Large Coaster

Materials:

Medium Weight Yarn (approximately 25 yards of main color and small amount of contrasting color)

Crochet Hook I (5.50 mm)

crochet yarn size 4

Instructions

Round 1: with main color, ch 4, 12 dc in forth ch from hook, sl st in top of beginning ch-4 joining to beginning of round: 12 dc

Round 2: ch 3, 2 dc in each dc around, sl st in top of beginning ch-3 joining to beginning of round: 24 dc

Round 3: ch 3, (2 dc in next dc, dc in next dc) around, sl st in top of beginning ch-3 joining to beginning of round: 36 dc

Round 4: ch 3, (2 dc in next dc, dc in next 2 dc) around, sl st in top of beginning ch-3 joining to beginning of round: 48 dc

Round 5: change to contrasting color, ch 3, (2 dc in next dc, dc in next 3 dc) around, sl st in top of beginning ch-3 joining to beginning of round, finish off: 60 dc

June 7 Fingerless Gloves

Materials:

Medium Weight Yarn

Crochet Hook H (5.00 mm)

Yarn Needle   crochet yarn size 4

Instructions

Row 1: ch 34, dc in third ch form hook, dc in each ch across: 32 dc

Row 2 – 11: ch 2, turn, dc in each dc across: 32 dc

Use yarn needle to sew sides of glove together leaving a 2" (5 cm) hole 1" (2.5 cm) from the end.

June 8 Soda Can Cozy

Materials:

Approximately 10 plastic bags made into plarn (plastic yarn)

Crochet hook H (5.00 mm)

Instructions

Round 1: ch 2, 6 sc in second ch from hook, place marker: 6 sc

Round 2: 2 sc in each sc around: 12 sc

Round 3: (2 sc in next sc, sc in next sc) around: 18 sc

Round 4: (2 sc in next sc, sc in next 2 sc) around: 24 sc

Round 5: (2 sc in next sc, sc in next 3 sc) around: 30 sc

Note: your circle should be 2 3/4" (7 cm) in diameter fitting perfectly under your soda can. After round 8, the bottom of your can should fit tightly into the cozy.

Round 6 – 20: sc in each sc around: 30 sc

June 9 Coffee Cup Sleeve

Materials:

Medium Weight Yarn (approximately 50 yards)

Crochet Hook G (4.00 mm)   crochet yarn size 4

Instructions

Round 1: ch 40, or a chain that is fits tightly around your coffee cup, sl st in first ch made, forming a loop and being carful not to twist chain: 40 ch

Round 2: ch 2, hdc in each ch around, sl st in top of beginning ch-2: 40 hdc

Round 3: ch 2, turn, hdc in each hdc around, sl st in top of beginning ch-2: 40 hdc

Repeat round 3, 6 times or until sleeve is as tall as you desire, then finish off.

June 10 Amazing Pillow Pattern

Materials

7 Balls cotton yarn

Steel Crochet Hook No. 2/0

Instructions

Ch 16 inches long.

1st row: Sc in 2nd ch from hook, * dc in next ch, sc in next ch. Repeat from * across until row measures 14 inches, ending with sc.

Cut off remaining chain. Ch 1, turn. 2nd row: Sc in each sc across. Ch 1, turn. 3rd row: Sc in first sc, * dc around bar of dc 2 rows below (raised dc), skip sc directly behind raised dc, sc in next sc. Repeat from * across. Ch 1, turn.

Repeat 2nd and 3rd rows alternately until piece is square. Break off.

June 11 Oriental Pillow Pattern

Materials

7 balls cotton yarn

Steel Crochet Hook No. 2/0

Instructions

Ch 16

1st row: Sc in 2nd ch from hook and in each ch across until row measures 14 inches, having a number of sc divisible by 3 and 2 more at end of row.

Cut off remaining chain. Ch 1, turn. 2nd row: Sc in first sc, skip next 2 sc, * tr in next sc, sc in each of the 2 skipped sc, skip next 2 free sc. Repeat from * across, ending with sc in last sc. Ch 1, turn. 3rd row: 2 sc in first sc (1 sc increased), sc in each st across to within last 2 sts, dec 1 sc—to dec 1 sc, work off last 2 sts as 1 sc. Ch 1, turn.

Repeat 2nd and 3rd rows alternately until piece is square, ending with the 3rd row. Break off

June 12 Frills Pillow Pattern

7 cotton yarn

Steel Crochet Hook No. 2/0

Ch 16 inches. 1st row: Sc in 2nd ch from hook and in each ch across until row measures 14 inches having a number of sc divisible by 4 and 2 more at end of row.

Cut off remaining chain. Ch 1, turn. 2nd row: Sc in first 2 sc, * tr in next sc, sc in next 3 sc. Repeat from * across, ending with tr in next sc, sc in last 2 sc. Ch 1, turn.

3rd row: Sc in each st across. Ch 1, turn. 4th row: Sc in first sc, * tr around bar of next tr 2 rows below (raised tr made), skip next sc, sc in next sc, raised tr around bar of same tr as first raised tr was made (raised V st made), skip next sc, sc in next sc.

Repeat from * across. Ch 1, turn. 5th row: Sc in each st across. Ch 1, turn. Repeat 2nd to 5th rows incl until piece is square.

June 13 Elizabethan rose tablecloth motif

Materials

Crochet Size 30

8½ yards of thread.

Instructions

Ch 8. Join with sl st to form ring. 1st rnd: 12 sc in ring. Join. 2nd rnd: Sc in same place as sl st, * ch 5, skip 1 sc, sc in next sc.

Repeat from * around. Join. 3rd rnd: In each loop around make sc, half dc, 5 dc, half dc and sc. Join. 4th rnd: * Ch 7, sc in back loop of sc between this and next petal. Repeat from * around.

Join. 5th rnd: In each loop around make sc, half dc, 7 dc, half dc and sc. Join. 6th rnd: Sl st to 2nd dc of first petal, sc in same place, * ch 5, skip 3 dc, sc in next dc, ch 5, sc in 2nd dc of next petal.

Repeat from * around. Join. 7th rnd: Sl st in next sp, ch 4, 2 tr in same sp, * ch 3, sc in top of last tr made (picot made), ch 12, sc in 3rd ch from hook (another picot made), 3 tr in same sp, ch 3, sc in next sp, picot, ch 10, picot, sc in next sp, ch 3, 3 tr in next sp. Repeat from * around. Join and break off.

June 14 Studio Couch Pillow pattern

Materials

Canary Yellow Cotton.

Steel Crochet Hook No. 2/

6½ yards dark green thread

Ch to reach tightly around narrow end of cushion

Join, being careful not to twist.

1st rnd: Sc in each ch around, do not join rnds.

2nd rnd: * Sc at base of next sc (long sc made), sc in back loop of next sc. Repeat from * around, ending with long sc. 3rd rnd: * Sc in back loop of next long sc, long sc at base of next sc.

Repeat from * around. Continue to work in pattern until piece measures same length as cushion. Sl st in next 2 sts and break off.

June 15 Bath Mat Pattern

24 balls of cotton yarn

Steel Crochet Hook No. 2/0

Ch 134 to measure 22 inches.

1st row: Sc in 2nd ch from hook, * tr in next ch, sc in next ch. Repeat from * across. Ch 1, turn. 2nd row: Sc in each st across. Ch 1, turn.

3rd row: Sc in first sc, tr around bar of 2nd tr on first row, skip 1 sc on row in work, sc in next sc, tr around bar of first tr on first row, * skip next sc on row in work, sc in next sc, skip next tr on first row, tr around bar of next tr, skip 1 sc, sc in next sc, tr around bar of skipped tr.

Repeat from * across. Ch 1, turn. Repeat 2nd and 3rd rows alternately until piece measures 34 inches.

June 16 Fathers' Day Classic Cotton Belt

100% mercerized cotton; 1 3/4 oz. (50 g); 108 yds.

2 skeins (burgundy MC)

Sizes E/4 (3.5 mm) crochet hook

Blunt-end yarn needle

Instructions

With MC, ch 9.

Row 1: Starting in 2nd ch from hook, sc in each ch across - - 8 sc. Ch 1, turn.

Row 2: Sc in each sc across. Ch 1, turn.

Rep Row 2 until Belt measures approx 28 inches or desired length. Keep in mind that to be worn as shown, Belt should be about 6 to 8 inches less than total hip measurement.

June 17 Beautiful Leaves

Materials

100% mercerized cotton (100 m)

Sizes E/4 (3.5 mm) crochet hook

Blunt-end yarn needle

1 skein chocolate

Instruction

Ch 7.

Row 1 (RS): Starting in 2nd ch from hook, sc in each of next 5 ch, 3 sc in last ch; working along opposite edge of foundation ch, sc in each of next 5 sts. Ch 1, turn.

Row 2: Sk first sc, working in back lp only, sc in each of next 5 sc, 3 sc in next sc, sc in each of next 5 sc. Ch 1, turn.

Row 3: Work as for Row 2. Fasten off.

June 18 Belt Design

Materials

American Thread 70 yd. skein of any 3 colors

Aluminum Crochet Hook, Size J

Instructions

Work a chain 2 yards long, cut yarn.

With right side of ch facing, attach yarn 18 inches from one end, sl st in each st to within 18 inches from opposite end, cut yarn.

Work 1 of each color.

With wrong side of strips facing, sew the 3 strips securely tog at beg of sl st sections, * braid for 4 inches, fasten securely; then sew the 3 strips tog again 6 inches from end of braided section; repeat from * once, braid for 4 inches, fasten securely.

Leave an 18 inch length of each color; if necessary shorten length of remaining ch ripping out remaining sl sts. Knot end of each ch.

June 19 Tartsy Bookmarks

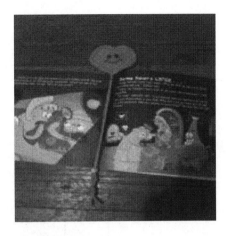

Materials

Worsted weight yarn

Pony bead

G Hook

Yarn needle

Craft eyes that snap on

Instruction

Rnd 1) Ch 2, 6 sc in 2nd ch from hook (6)

Rnd 2) 2 sc in each st around (12)

Rnd 3) (sc in next st, 2 sc in next st) repeat around (18)

Rnd 4) (sc in next 2 sts, 2 sc in next st) repeat around (24)

Fasten off.

June 20 Holly Bookmark

Materials

Size 10 Crochet thread

Size 7 Steel crochet hook

Needle with eye large enough to accept thread

Red seed beads for holly berries

Instructions

Leaf

Ch 10, sc in 2nd ch from hook, *hdc in next ch, dc in next ch, picot, dc in next ch, hdc in next ch, dc in next ch, picot, dc in next ch, hdc in next ch*, sc in last ch, picot, sc in same st. Working in the unused loops of foundation ch and over the tail, repeat from * to *, sc in last ch, slipstitch in first sc.

Tail

Ch 69, sc in 10th ch from hook, to form ring. Sc in each chain, slipstitch in same st as first ch. DO NOT fasten off

June 21 Facecloth

Materials

100-300 Yards Cotton Yarn.

Size H Crochet Hook

Scissors

Instructions

Chain 21

Row 1:   Turn, Sc in 2nd Ch from hook and each stitch across to end. = 20 Sc

Row 2:   Turn, Ch 1, Sc in 1st St, Skip next Stitch, *Sc, Ch 2, Sc all in the next stitch. Skip next 2 Stitches*, Repeat * * across to the last 2 stitches. Skip stitch and Sc in the last stitch. = 6 Chain 2 Spaces and 1 Sc on each end.

Row 3: Turn, Ch 3 (Counts as DC), 3 Dc in next Ch 2 Space (Dc Cluster made). Repeat Dc Cluster in each Ch 2 space across. Dc in last stitch. = 6 Dc Clusters and 1 Dc on each end.

Row 4-11: Repeat rows 2 & 3 four more times.

June 22 Big Bob Washcloth

Materials

300 Yards Cotton Yarn.

Size H Crochet Hook

Scissors

Instructions

Chain 27

Row 1:   Turn, Sc in 2nd Ch from hook and each stitch across to end. = 26 Sc

Row 2: Turn, Ch 1, Sc in 1st St, Skip next Stitch, *Sc, Ch 2, Sc all in the next stitch. Skip next 2 Stitches*, Repeat * * across to the last 2 stitches. Skip stitch and Sc in the last stitch. = 8 Chain 2 Spaces and 1 Sc on each end.

Row 3: Turn, Ch 3 (Counts as DC), 3 Dc in next Ch 2 Space (Dc Cluster made). Repeat Dc Cluster in each Ch 2 space across. Dc in last stitch. = 8 Dc Clusters and 1 Dc on each end.

Row 4-15: Repeat rows 2 & 3 Six more times.

June 23 Hand Towel

Materials

100 Yards Cotton Yarn.

Size H Crochet Hook

Scissors

Instruction

Row 1: Turn, Sc in 2nd Ch from hook and each stitch across to end. = 32 Sc

Row 2: Turn, Ch 1, Sc in 1st St, Skip next Stitch, *Sc, Ch 2, Sc all in the next stitch. Skip next 2 Stitches*, Repeat * * across to the last 2 stitches. Skip stitch and Sc in the last stitch. = 10 Chain 2 Spaces and 1 Sc on each end.

Row 3: Turn, Ch 3 (Counts as DC), 3 Dc in next Ch 2 Space (Dc Cluster made). Repeat Dc Cluster in each Ch 2 space across. Dc in last stitch. = 10 Dc Clusters and 1 Dc on each end.

Row 4-21: Repeat rows 2 & 3 Nine more times.

June 24 Alora Earrings

Materials:

Fine Weight Yarn

Crochet Hook C (2.75 mm)

2 earwires

Crochet yarn size 2

Instructions

Row 1: ch 8, 2 sc in second ch from hook and each ch across: 14 sc

Row 2:ch 5, turn, skip 2 sc, sl st in next sc, ch 5, skip 1 sc, sl st in next sc, ch 5, skip 1 sc, hdc2tog, (ch 5, skip 1 sc, sl st in next sc) across: 36 sts

Row 3: ch 1, turn, sc in first 4 sts, (ch 5, skip 5 sts, sc in next st) 2 times, ch 6, skip 5 sts, sc in next st, (ch 5, skip 5 sts, sc in next st) 2 times, sc in last 2 sts: 37 sts

Finish off.

Add earwires.

June 25 Coffeemaker Cozy

Materials:

Light Weight Yarn

Crochet hook G (4.00 mm)

Instructions

First side

Row 1: ch 25, sc in second ch from hook and in each ch across: 24 sc

Row 2: ch 1, turn, (sc in next 6 sc, 2 sc in next sc) 3 times, sc in last 3 sc: 27 sc

Row 3: ch 1, turn, (sc in next 7 sc, 2 sc in next sc) 3 times, sc in last 3 sc: 30 sc

Row 4: ch 1, turn, (sc in next 8 sc, 2 sc in next sc) 3 times, sc in last 3 sc: 33 sc

Row 5: ch 1, turn, (sc in next 9 sc, 2 sc in next sc) 3 times, sc in last 3 sc: 36 sc

Row 6: ch 1, turn, (sc in next 10 sc, 2 sc in next sc) 3 times, sc in last 3 sc: 39 sc

Row 8: ch 1, turn, (sc in next 11 sc, 2 sc in next sc) 3 times, sc in last 3 sc: 42 sc

Finish off.

Second side

On opposite side of foundation chain, join yarn in first sc,

Row 1: ch 1, turn, sc in each ch across: 24 sc

Row 2 – 8: repeat Rows 2 – 8 of first side.

Finish off.

June 26 Open Cuff Bracelet

Materials:

Medium Weight Yarn (approximately 10 yards)

Crochet Hook J (6.00 mm)   crochet yarn size 4

Instruction

Round 1: ch 17, sc in second ch from hook, (ch 4, skip 4 ch, sc in next ch) 3 times: 28 sts

Round 2: (8 sc in next ch-space, skip next sc) 2 times, 8 sc in next ch-space, 3 sc in next sc, (8 sc in next ch-space, skip next sc) 2 times, 8 sc in next ch-space, sl st in next sc, ch 5: 51 sc

Finish off. To close the bracelet, weave the chain through the small hole in the other end of the bracelet.

June 27 Upside Down Earrings

Materials:

Size 5 thread (approximately 5 yards)

Crochet Hook C (2.75 mm)

33 seed beads crochet yarn size 0

Instructions

Row 1: Make adjustable ring, ch 1, sc with bead: 1 sc

Row 2: ch 1, turn, 3 sc in sc: 3 sc

Row 3: ch 1, turn, sc with bead in each sc across: 3 sc

Row 4: ch 1, turn, 2 sc in first sc, sc in next sc, 2 sc in last sc: 5 sc

Row 5: ch 1, turn, sc with bead in each sc across: 5 sc

Row 6: ch 1, sc in first 2 sc, 3 sc in next sc, sc in last 2 sc: 7 sc

Row 7: ch 1, turn, sc with bead in each sc across: 7 sc

Row 8: turn, sl st in each sc across: 7 sl st

Row 9: turn, ch 3, tr with bead in each sl st across, sl st in last sl st: 7 tr

Finish off. Add ear wire.

June 28 Fresh Floral Face Cloth

Materials:

Medium Weight Yarn

Crochet Hook J (6.00 mm)

Crochet yarn size 4

Instructions

Round 1: make adjustable ring, ch 2, 8 hdc in ring, sl st in first hdc: 8 hdc

Round 2: 2 hdc in each hdc around, sl st in first hdc: 16 hdc

Round 3: (2 hdc in next hdc, hdc in next hdc) around, sl st in first hdc: 24 hdc

Round 4: ch 3, dc in next hdc, 2 tr in next 2 hdc, (dc, ch 3, sl st) in next hdc, ([sl st, ch 3, dc] in next hdc, 2 tr in each of next 2 hdc, [dc, ch 3, sl st] in next hdc) around: 48 sts

Finish off.

June 29 Dish Soap Apron

Materials:

Medium Weight Yarn 30:10 color A : color B

Crochet Hook J (6.00 mm)   crochet yarn size 4

Instructions

Row 1: with color A, ch 12, hdc in third ch from hook and in each ch across: 10 hdc

Row 2 – 12: ch 2, turn, hdc in each hdc across: 10 hdc

Row 13: ch 2, turn, hdc2tog, hdc in next 6 hdc, hdc2tog: 8 hdc

Row 14 – 15: ch 2, turn, hdc in each hdc across: 8 hdc

Row 16: ch 2, turn, hdc2tog, hdc in next 4 hdc, hdc2tog: 6 hdc

Row 17: ch 2, turn, hdc in each hdc across: 6 hdc

Finish off.

June 30 Doll Basket

Materials:

Medium Weight Yarn (approximately 8 yards of main color, a small amount of contrasting color)

Crochet Hook H (5.00 mm)

crochet yarn size 4

Instructions

Round 1: with main color, make an adjustable ring, ch 1, 6 sc in ring, sl st in first sc: 6 sc

Round 2: ch 1, 2 sc in each sc around, sl st in first sc: 12 sc

Round 3: ch 1, sc in back loop only in each sc around, sl st in first sc: 12 sc

Round 4 – 5: ch 1, sc in each sc around, sl st in first sc: 12 sc

Round 6: ch 1, *2 sc in next sc, sc in next sc, repeat from * around, sl st in first sc: 18 sc

Round 7: ch 1, *2 sc in next sc, sc in next 2 sc, repeat from * around, sl st in first sc: 24 sc

Round 8: ch 1, sc in each sc around, sl st in first sc: 24 sc

Handle: ch 16, sl st in 13th sc,

Finish off.

July

July 1: Textured Washcloth

Materials:

Dk Weight Yarn

Crochet Hook H (5.00 mm)

Instructions

Row 1: ch 22, sl st in third ch from hook, (hdc in next ch, sl st in next ch) across, ending with a hdc in last ch: 10 hdc, 10 sl st

Row 2: ch 2, turn, sl st in first hdc, (hdc in next sl st, sl st in next hdc) across, ending with a hdc in beginning ch-2: 10 hdc, 10 sl st

Rows 3-20: Repeat Row 2

Finish off, weave in any ends!

July 2 Cleaning Pads

Materials:

Medium Weight Yarn

Crochet Hook J (6.00 mm)   crochet yarn size 4

Gauge: Rounds 1 – 2 in pattern creates a circle 2 3/4″ in diameter

Instructions

Round 1: ch 4, 12 dc in forth ch from hook, sl st in top of beginning ch-3: 12 dc

Round 2: ch 3, 2 dc in each dc around, sl st in top of beginning ch-3, finish off: 24 dc

July 3 Nano Cozy

Materials:

#10 Bedspread Weight Cotton Thread

Steel Hook Size 7

Yarn Needle

Instructions

R1: Ch23, sc in 2nd ch from hook. Sc in ea rem ch across to the last ch.

3sc in the last ch. Working along the opposite side of the foundation chain, sc in ea unworked lp of each foundation ch, placing 2 additional scs in the last ch for a total of 3sc on that end. Join with a sl st.

R2: Ch1, do not turn. Sc in BL of ea sc around. Join with sl st.

R3: Ch1, do not turn. Sc in ea sc around. Do not join.

July 4 Crochet Rib Mug Cozy

Materials

100% cotton yarn

Hook: 4.5mm

Instructions

Make a chain of 13 stitches. Turn,

In the second stitch from the Hook working through the back strand only, work a row of Double crochet, 1 chain to turn at the end of the row.

Repeat this row, changing color as required until your cozy will stretch around your mug. Remember rib is stretchy.

Work two rows of double crochet loosely and evenly around the whole cozy to finish off.

July 5 Granny Stripe Cup Cozy

Materials

4.5 mm hook

100% cotton yarn

Instructions

Make a chain to fit around your mug with multiples of 3 plus 1 ch for turning.

Work the foundation row by making 3 trb into the second stitch from the hook and then every alternate stitch along the row. 1 chain to turn.

Change color and make 3 ch, make three trb into each cluster space of the previous row to the end, end with 1 treble in the last stitch, 1 ch to turn.

Repeat these two row three times. Work 1 more row to end with your main color.

July 6 Mug Tie Cozy

Materials

Yarn Cotton, medium worsted

Hook: Size (I-9) 5.5 mm

Instructions

Ch 12.

Row 1: Sc in 2nd ch from hook and in ea rem ch. (11 sc)

Rows 2 – 26: Ch 1, turn, sc in ea st across. (11 sc)

Do not finish off.

Begin where you left off final row.

Row 1: Sc in same st, sc at the end of each row along the side of cozy, 2 sc in corner, sc in ea of the next 5 sts of short side of cozy, ch 30, sk 1 st, sc in ea of the next st 5 sts, 2 sc in corner, sc at the end of each row along other side of cozy, 2 sc in corner, sc in ea of the next 5 sts of short side of cozy, ch 30, sk 1 st, sc in ea of the next 5 sts, sl st in next st, finish off, weave in ends.

July 7 Kindle Sleeve

Materials

Universal Yarn

4.0mm hook

Yarn needle

Instructions

Ch 24.

1. Dc in 3rd ch from hook, *sk 2 ch, (sc, 2dc) in next ch. Rep from * across to last 3 chs. Sk next 2 chs, sc in last ch. Ch 1, turn.

2. (Sc, 2dc) in first sc. *Sk next 2 dc, (sc, 2dc) in next sc. Rep from * across to last 3 sts. Sk next 2 sts, sc in last st. Ch 1, turn (25 sts).

3. Rep row 2 until piece measures 14 1/2 inches from beg.

July 8 Warm Hat

Materials

1 skein Red Heart Baby Clouds

M (9.0 mm) hook

Instructions

Ch 28.

1. Hdc in 3rd ch from hook (2 chs count as first hdc, now and throughout), hdc in each ch across. Ch 2, turn (26 hdc).

2. Working in blo, hdc in each st across. Ch 2, turn (26 hdc).

3. Repeat row 2 until piece measures approx. 19 1/2 inches from beg.

Sc ends tog and gather at the top. FO. Turn right side out and turn up brim.

July 9 Ear Warmer

Materials

1 ball James C. Brett Marble

Set of size 6 DPNs

Yarn needle

Instructions

Cast on 27 sts. Distribute evenly over 3 dpn's.

Knit one round, place marker.

Knit around until piece measures approx. 19 ½ inches from beg. FO, leaving a long tail.

Stitch ends together.

July 10 Fusion Throw

Materials

Lion Brand Jiffy, 7 balls (3.5 oz) each:

CA (Shocking Pink)

CB (Apple Green)

CC (Aqua)

Q (15.0 mm) hook

P (11.5 mm) hook

Instructions

With Q hook and CA and CB held together, ch 86.

1. Hdc in 3rd ch from hook and each ch across (84 hdc). Ch 1, turn.

2. Hdc in each ch across. Cut CA, join CC (84 hdc). Ch 1, turn.

3, 4. With CC and CB held tog, hdc in each st across. At end of row 4, cut CB, join CA. Ch 1, turn (84 hdc).

5, 6. With CA and CC held together, hdc in each st across, ch 1, turn. At end of row six, cut CC, join CB. Ch 1, turn.

Continue working in established pattern (hdc in each across, ch 1, turn) in following color scheme:

*(2 rows CA and CB; 2 rows CC and CB; 2 rows CA and CC.)

Repeat * until piece measures approximately 48 inches from beg, FO.

July 11 iPod Cozy

Materials

1 ball I Love This Cotton

1 small button

F (3.5 mm) hook

Yarn needle

Instructions

Ch. 17

1. Sc in first ch, dc in next ch. (Sc in next ch, dc in next ch) across. Ch 1, turn (16 sts).

2. Sc in first st, dc in next st. (Sc in next st, dc in next st) across. Ch 1, turn (16 sts).

3. Repeat row 2 until piece measures 4 ¼ inches from beg. Ch 1, turn.

4. Sl st in first 4 sts, ch 14, sl st in next 4 sts. FO. **Note: the number of chains can be varied to accommodate different sized buttons.**

July 12 Scarf Striped

Materials

1 ball Lion Brand Wool Ease Color A (black)

1 ball Lion Brand Wool Ease Color B (white/multi)

1 ball Lion Brand Wool Ease Color C (grey heather)

Size 7 needles

Instructions

With CA, cast on 20.

Rows 1 - 6: Knit across, switch to CB.

7, 8: Knit across, switch to CC.

9 - 14: Knit across, switch to CA.

15, 16: Knit across, switch to CB.

17 - 22: Knit across, switch to CC.

23, 24: Knit across, switch to CA.

Repeat rows 1 – 24 until piece measures approximately 47 to 47.5 inches from beg.

Repeat rows 1 – 6.

FO, weave in ends.

July 13 Keyhole Scarf

Materials

1 skein Lion Brand Homespun Color A

1 skein Lion Brand Homespun Color B

1 ball Sirdar Zanzibar

K (6.5 mm) hook

Instructions

With 1 strand A and 1 strand Zanzibar held together, ch 15.

1. Hdc in 3rd ch from hook and each ch across. Ch 1, turn (13 hdc).

2. Hdc in each ch across. Ch 1, turn (13 hdc).

Repeat row 2 until piece measures 13 inches from beginning. Cut Homespun CA, join CB.

Holding Homespun and Zanzibar tog, repeat row 2 until piece measures approximately 22 inches from beg.

3. Hdc in first 2 sts, ch 9, hdc in last 2 sts.

4. Hdc in each hdc and ch across. Ch 1, turn (13 hdc).

Repeat row 2 until piece measures 26 inches from beg. FO, add fringe.

July 14 Triple Warm Ear Warmer

Materials

1 Skein Caron Simply Soft Yarn

Matching thread

Scrap of fleece 22 inches by 3 inches.

G (4.0) hook

Sewing needle

Yarn needle

Instructions

Ch 32. Being careful not to twist, join ends with a sl st.

1. Ch 1. Sc in same ch and each ch around. Join to first sc with sl st (32 sc).

2. Ch 1, sc in same st and each st around. Join (32 sc).

Repeat row 2 until piece measures 22 ½ inches. Cut yarn.

Stitch ends together, FO.

July 15 Slide-In iPod Nano Sleeve

Materials

1 ball Noro Kureyon

G (4.0mm) hook

Yarn needle

Instructions

Ch 9.

1. Sc in each ch across. Working in unused loops of foundation ch, sc in each ch across. Join with sl st to first sc. (16 sc).

2. Ch 1, sc in each sc around, join with sl st to first sc.

Repeat row 2 until piece measures approx. 4 inches from beg. Ch 1, turn (16 sc).

3. Ch 1, sc in next 8 sc. Ch 1, turn (8 sc).

4-8. Repeat row 3.

9. Sc first 2 sc tog, sc in next 4 sc, sc last 2 sc tog. Ch 1, turn (6 sc).

10. Sc first 2 sc tog, sc in next 2 sc, sc last 2 sc tog. Ch 1, turn (4 sc).

11. Sc first 2 sc tog, sc last 2 sc tog, FO (2 sc).

July 16 Wannabe Scarf

Materials

2 balls Lion Suede

1 ball Bernat Soft Boucle

K (6.5) hook

J (6.0) hook

Instructions

With Lion Suede and K hook, ch 13.

1. Sc in 2nd ch from hook and each ch across. Ch 1, turn (12 sc).

2. Sc in each sc across. Ch 1, turn (12 sc).

3. Repeat row 2 until piece measures approx. 50 ½ inches. FO.

July 17 Easy Dish Cloth

Materials:

size 9 (5.5 mm) afghan hook

100% cotton yarn

Instructions

Chain as many as you wish until it is as wide as you want your dishcloth.

Row 1: Insert hook in the back of 2nd ch from hook, work afghan stitch across

The rest of the rows: continue working afghan stitch until your piece is square.

Finish off: ch 1, sc across.

July 18 Filet Dad Bookmark

Materials:

Size 7 steel hook

size 10 bedspread weight thread.

Instructions

Note: The ch 3 at end of row counts as first dc in next row throughout.

Starting at bottom, ch 22.

Row 1: Dc in 4th ch from hook and in next 8 ch, ch 2, skip 2 ch, dc in next 9 chs, ch 3, turn. (18 dc, 1 ch-2 sp)

Row 2: Dc in next 8 dc, 2 dc in ch-2 sp, dc in next 9 dc, ch 3, turn. (20 dc)

Row 3: Dc in next 2 dc, (ch 2, skip 2 dc, dc in next dc) 4 times, ch 2, dc in last 3 dc, ch 3, turn. (10 dc, 5 ch-2 sps)

Row 4: Dc in next 2 dc, ch 2, dc in next dc, (2 dc in next ch-2 sp, dc in next dc) 3 times, ch 2, dc in last 3 dc, ch 3, turn. (16 dc, 2 ch-2 sps)

Row 5: Dc in next 2 dc, ch 2, dc in next 4 dc, ch 2, skip 2 dc, dc in next 4 dc, ch 2, dc in last 3 dc, ch 3, turn.

Rows 6-9: Dc in next 2 dc, (ch 2,dc in next 4 dc) twice, ch 2, dc in last 3 dc, ch 3, turn. (14 dc, 3 ch-2 sps)

Row 10: Dc in next 2 dc, ch 2, dc in next 4 dc, 2 dc in ch-2 sp, dc in next 4 dc, ch 2, dc in last 3 dc, ch 3, turn. (16 dc, 2 ch-2 sps)

Row 11: Dc in next 2 dc, ch 2, (dc in next dc, ch 2, sk 2 dc) 4 times, dc in last 3 dc, ch 3, turn. (10 dc, 5 ch-2 sps)

Row 12: Dc in next 2 dc, ch 2, (dc in next dc, ch 2) 4 times, dc in last 3 dc, ch 3, turn.

Row 13: Dc in next 2 dc, * ch 2, dc in next dc, 2 dc in ch-2 sp, dc in next dc *, repeat between * once, ch 2, dc in last 3 dc, ch 3, turn. (14 dc, 3 ch-2 sps)

Rows 14-15: Dc in next 2 dc (ch 2, dc in next 4 dc) twice, ch 2, dc in last 3 dc, ch 3, turn.

Row 16: Repeat row 10.

Row 17: Dc in next 2 dc, ch 2, * dc in next 4 dc, ch 2 *, skip 2 dc, repeat between * once, dc in last 3 dc, ch 3, turn.

Row 18: Repeat row 6.

Row 19: Repeat row 10.

Row 20: Repeat row 11.

Row 21: Repeat row 12.

Row 22: Repeat row 4.

Row 23: Repeat row 5.

Rows 24-27: Repeat row 6.

Row 28: Repeat row 10.

Row 29: Repeat row 11.

Row 30: Dc in next 2 dc, (2 dc in ch-2 sp, dc in next dc) 4 times, 2 dc in ch-2 sp, dc in next 3 dc, ch 3, turn. (20 dc)

Row 31: Dc in each dc across. Fasten off.

July 19 Bug Scrubbie

Materials:

polyester rug yarn

"I" hook

Instructions

Row 1: Ch 20 loosely.Sc in 2nd ch from hook and in each ch across(19 sc).

Row 2: Ch 1,turn.Sc in each st across.

Row 3-29: Rep row 2.Do not finish off.

July 20 Mesh Soap Saver

Materials:

Size I (5.5mm) Crochet Hook

Size H (5.omm) Crochet Hook

Worsted Weight Yarn

35 yds of Color A

1 yd of Color B.

Yarn Needle, for weaving ends

Instructions:

With I Hook

Ch 11

Row 1: Sc in 2nd ch from hook, and in each ch across. Turn. (10)

Row 2: Ch 1, sc in each st across. Turn. (10)

Row 3/Round 3: Ch 1, 2 sc in the first st, sc in each st until the last st of the row, 2 sc in the last st of the row. Work 3 sc down the side of the rows. Working in the bottom loops of the original chain, 2 sc in first ch, sc in each ch until the last ch, 2 sc in the last ch. Work 3 sc up the side of the rows. Join in first sc. Do not turn. You will now be working in the round. (30)

Round 4: Ch 4 (counts as dc and ch 1), sk next st *dc in next st, ch 1, sk next st** Repeat from * to ** around. Join in top of t-ch. (15 dcs)

Round 5: Ch 4 (counts as dc and ch 1), *dc in ch-1 sp, ch 1** Repeat from * to ** around. Join in top of t-ch. (15 dcs)

Rounds 6-9: Repeat Round 5

Round 10: ch 1, hdc in each ch-1 sp and in the top of each dc around. Fasten off, join using an invisible join. (30)

July 21 Tatting A 3-Color Flower

Materials

2 shuttles, each wound with a different color

1 ball of a third color

1 small rubber band (optional: for holding shuttles together while tatting chains)

Instructions

Note which color of thread will be shuttle 1 vs. shuttle 2.

With Shuttle 1: R 3-3-3-3 (Cl R and RW after each Ring)

Add Shuttle 2 thread and Ball thread to pinch.

Begin a chain, tatting with both shuttle threads as base thread:

Ch 4-4-4 (RW after each Chain)

*With Shuttle 2: R 3+3-3-3

Ch 4-4-4 (tatting with both shuttle threads, as before)

With Shuttle 1: R 3+3-3-3

Ch 4-4-4 (tatting with both shuttle threads)

Repeat from * 2 more times.

With Shuttle 2: R 3+3-3+3

Ch 4-4-4 (tatting with both shuttle threads)

July 22 Medium Motif

Materials

2 shuttles, each wound with a different color

1 ball of a third color

1 small rubber band (optional: for holding shuttles together while tatting chains)

Instructions

* Ch 7 rw

   R 5 - 5 rw

   Ch 3 - 3 - 3 - 3 rw

   R 5 + 5 rw

   Ch 3 - 3 - 3 - 3 rw

   R 5 + 5 rw

   Ch 3 - 3 - 3 - 3 rw

   R 5 + 5 rw

   Ch 3 - 3 - 3 - 3 rw

   R 5 + 5 rw

   Ch 7 rw

   R 5 - 5 rw

Repeat from "*" for the amount of medium motifs you desire. This example has 8 motifs.

July 23 Large Motif

Materials

2 shuttles, each wound with a different color

1 ball of a third color

1 small rubber band (optional: for holding shuttles together while tatting chains)

Instructions

* Ch 10 rw

   R   6 - 6 rw (make picot large enough for 4 joins)

   Ch 3 - 3 - 3 - 3 - 3 rw

   R   6 + 6 rw

   Ch 3 - 3 - 3 - 3 - 3 rw

   R   6 + 6 rw

   Ch 3 - 3 - 3 - 3 - 3 rw

   R   6 +6 rw

   Ch 3 - 3 - 3 - 3 - 3 rw

   R   6 + 6 rw

   Ch 10

   R   5 + 5 rw

July 24 Alice Insertion

Materials

Size 60 Coats mercer crochet cotton.

Appropriate crochet hook

Instructions

First Row

Clover:

Ring: 10ds, p, 10ds

Ring: 10ds, p, 10ds

Ring: 10ds, p, 10ds

* Chain: 5ds, 3p sep 5ds, 5ds

Clover:

Ring: 10ds, join to p of 2nd Ring of previous clover, 10ds

Ring: 10ds, p, 10ds

Ring: 10ds, p, 10ds

Second Row

Clover:

Ring: 10ds, join to free p of second ring of first clover, 10ds

Ring: 10ds, join between first two clovers of first row, 10ds

Ring: 10ds, join to free p of second ring of second clover, 10ds

* Chain: 5ds, 3p sep 5ds, 5ds

Clover:

Ring: 10ds, join to + of last ring on previous clover, 10ds

Ring: 10ds, join between next two clovers of first row, 10ds

Ring: 10ds, join to free p of second ring of next clover, 10ds

July 25 Blue Doily

Materials

Crochet cotton size 30

Crochet hook appropriate

Row 1

* Lrg R   4 - 4 -- 4 - 4 rw (make middle picot long enough for 3 joins)

Ch   5 - 5 rw

Sm R   3 + 3 - 3 rw (join to picot of previous ring)

Ch   5 - 5 rw

Continue around from " * " until there are 4 Large and 4 Small rings. Join to base of first ring and chain, cut and tie.

Row 2

* R   5 - 5 rw

   Ch 6 + 6 rw (join to picot of previous row)

   R   5 - 5 rw

Continue around from " * " until there are 8 rings. Join to base of first ring and chain, cut and tie.

Row 3

R   5 + 5 rw (join to picot of previous row)

* Ch   3 - 3 rw

R   5 + 5 rw (join to same picot of privous row)

Ch   3 - 5 - 5 - 3 rw

R   5 + 5 rw (join to next picot of previous row)

Continue around from " * " joining 2 rings to each picot of previous row. Join to base of first ring and chain, cut and tie.

Row 4

R   3 - 3 + 3 - 3 rw (join to middle picot of long chain.

* Ch   5 - 5 - 5 rw

R   3 - 3 + 3 - 3 rw (join to picot of small chain)

Continue around from " * " joining to previous row. Join to base of first ring and chain, cut and tie.

Row 5

* R   5 + 5 rw (join to picot of previous row)

Short Ch   4 - 4 rw

R   5 + 5 rw (join to picot of privous row)

Long Ch   4 - 4 - 4 rw

Continue around from " * " join to previous row. Join to base of first ring and chain, cut and tie.

Row 6

* R   5 + 5 rw (join to picot of previous row)

   Ch 4 - 4 rw

Continue around from " * " joining to previous row. Join to base of first ring and chain, cut and tie.

July 26 Blue Motif Pattern

Materials

100% cotton yarn

Appropriate hook

Instructions

5 ds ,4 p sep by 3 ds,5 ds, CL.

5 ds,join p to last p of previous ring, 6 p sep by 3 ds,5 ds,CL.

5 ds, join p to last p of previous ring,3 p sep by 3 ds,5 ds. CL RW

Chain : 15 ds. RW

Repeat the clover a total of 4 times. Join together

July 27 Sampler Square

Materials:

3 ounces of worsted weight yarn, I hook

Instructions:

ch 41

Row 1 - skip 1st 2 chs (counts as 1st hdc) *sl st in next ch, hdc in next ch* repeat from *to * across ending with a sl st in the last ch, turn

Row 2 - ch 2(counts as 1st hdc) sk 1st st, *sl st into next hdc, hdc in next sl st* repeat from * to) across ending with a sl st in the top of the turning ch, turn

repeat row 2 until your piece measures 12 inches and fasten off

July 28 Tilted Square

Materials:

Size I (or any size) hook, any color 4 ply worsted yarn.

Instructions

Ch 5, and join to form a ring.

Rnd 1: Ch 3 (counts as first dc here and throughout), 2 dc, ch 2, * 3 dc, ch 2; repeat from * 2 more times, join to top of beg ch 3.

Rnd 2: Sl st between next 2 dc, ch 3, dc between next 2 dc, * 2 dc, ch 2, 2 dc in next ch 2 sp (corner made), dc between dc (twice); repeat from * twice more; 2 dc, ch 2, 2 dc in next ch 2 sp, join to top of beg ch 3.

Rnd 3: Ch 6, * sk 1 st, dc, ch 3, repeat from * around, join with sl st to 3rd ch of beg ch 6.

Rnd 4: Sl st to next ch 3 sp, ch 3, 2dc in same sp, 3 dc in next sp, 3 dc ch 2, 3 dc in corner sp, * 3 dc in each ch 3 sp across sides, 3 dc, ch 2, 3 dc in corner sp, repeat from * twice more; 3 dc in next ch-3 sp, join to top of beg ch 3, end off

July 29 Window Square

Materials:

Size I hook; any color 4 ply worsted weight yarn.

Instructions

Ch 6, join.

Round 1: Ch 8, (dc into ring, ch 5) 3 times, join in 3rd ch of beg ch-8.

Round 2: Sl st into next ch-5 sp, ch 3, 4 dc, ch 2, 5 dc in same sp, (5 dc, ch 2 5 dc in next ch-5 sp) 3 times, join in top of beg ch-3.

Round 3: Ch 3, dc in next 4 sts, (2 dc, ch 2, 2 dc in corner sp, dc in next 10 sts) 3 times, 2 dc, ch 2, 2 dc in corner sp, dc in next 5 dc, join to top of beg ch-3.

Round 4: Ch 4, (sk 1 st, dc in next st, ch 1) 3 times, * 2 dc, ch 3, 2 dc in corner sp, (ch 1, sk 1 st, dc in next st) 7 times, ch 1, repeat from * 2 more times; 2 dc, ch 3, 2 dc in corner sp, (ch 1, sk 1 st, dc in next st) 3 times, ch 1, join to 3rd ch of beg ch-4, end off.

July 30 Bunny Finger Puppet

Materials:

Super Fine Yarn (approximately 10 yards)

Crochet Hook E (3.5 mm)

Instructions

Round 1: Make an adjustable ring, ch 1, 6 sc in ring, sl st in beg ch-1: 6 sc

Rounds 2-12: sc in each sc around

Finish off.

Ears (make 2):

Row 1: Ch 5, sc in second ch from hook and in each ch across: 4 sc

Finish off. Sew ears to top of body and embroider face to body.

July 31 Mug Cozy

Materials:

US size I9/5.5mm hook

1 Skein Bernat Softee Chunky in Natural

4 1-inch mismatched vintage buttons

Instructions

Row 1: Chain (ch) 2, this will always count as the first stitch. Crochet 11 double crochet (dc) into the loop, join last stitch to beginning chain stitch with a slip stitch (slst), and tighten the loop. (12 dc)

Row 2: Ch 2. 2dc in each dc, join with a slst. (24 dc)

Row 3: Ch 2. *2dc in first dc, 1 dc in next.* Repeat from * until end of row, join with a slst. (36 dc)

Row 4: Ch 1. Single crochet (sc) in each stitch around, join with a slst. (36 sc)

Row 5: Ch 2. Dc in the back loop only of each stitch around, join with a slst. (36 dc)

Row 6: Ch 2, turn. Dc in next 33 stitches. Do not join. (34 dc)

Rows 7-8: Repeat row 6. (34 dc)

Row 9: Ch 2, turn. Dc in next 33 stitches. (34 dc) Chain 9 and attach the end of the chain to the bottom of the dc with a ss. This will create the loop for the button closure.

Row 10: Slst. Remove hook from yarn and insert it thru the front top of the last dc. Draw yarn loop through top of stitch. For decorative edging: *sc in first dc, ch1, slst in next dc.* Repeat from * until end of row.

August
August 1 Autumn Harvest Scarf

Materials:

Medium Weight Yarn (approximately 280 yards)

Crochet hook J (6.00 mm)   crochet yarn size 4

Instructions

Row 1: ch 30, dc in sixth ch from hook, *skip 2 ch, 5 dc in next ch, skip 2 ch, dc in next ch, ch 1, skip 1 ch, dc in next ch, repeat from * across: 23 sts

Row 2: ch 4 (counts as 1 dc and 1 ch), turn, skip first dc, dc in next dc, *skip 2 dc, 5 dc in next dc, skip 2 dc, dc in next dc, ch 1, dc in next dc, repeat from * across: 23 sts

Repeat Row 2, 103 more times or until scarf is the desired length.

Finish off.

August 2 Block Tunisian Scarf for Barbie

Materials:

Fingering Weight Yarn (approximately 5 yards)

Crochet Hook G (4.00 mm)   crochet yarn size 1

Instructions

Row 1: ch 7, pull up loop in secon ch from hook and in each ch across

Return pass: ch 1, (yo, pull through two loops) until one loop remains on hook: 6 sts

Row 2-7: tks in each st across: 6 tks

Row 8-9: TSS in each st across: 6 TSS

Row 10-41: repeat rows 2-9, 4 times

Row 42-46: tks in eack st across: 6 tks

Finish off, slip stitching into each tks as if to tks.

August 3 Cable Bow

Materials:

Medium Weight Yarn (approximately 10 yards)

Crochet Hook G (4.0 mm)   crochet yarn size 4

Instructions

Row 1: ch 11, dc in fourth ch from hook and in each ch across: 8 dc

Row 2: ch 3, turn, fpdc in each dc across: 8 dc

Row 3: ch 3, turn, bpdc in each dc across: 8 dc

Row 4: repeat row 2

Row 5: Repeat row 3

Row 6: ch 3, skip 4 dc, fpdc in next dc and in next 3 dc, with hook in front of work, fpdc in first skipped dc and in next 3 dc: 8 dc

Row 7 – 10: repeat rows 3 and 4

Row 11: repeat row 3

Finish off.

August 4 Tripoint Bookmark

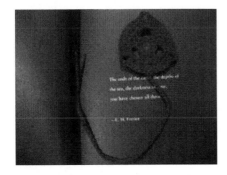

Materials:

Size 10 Thread (approximately 10 yards)

Crochet Hook B (2.25 mm)   crochet yarn size 0

Instructions

Round 1: make an adjustable ring, ch 3, 9 dc in ring, sl st in first dc: 9 dc

Round 2: ch 3, (2 dc in next dc, ch 3, skip 1 dc, 2 dc in next dc) around: 21 sts

Round 3: ch 3, (2 dc in next 2 dc, [2 dc, ch 3, 2 dc] in next ch-space, 2 dc in next 2 dc) around: 45 sts

Ch 50, then finish off.

August 5 Beanie for Barbie Doll

Materials:

Super Fine Weight Yarn (approximately 5 yards)

Crochet Hook C (2.75 mm)   crochet yarn size 1

Instructions

Round 1: Make an adjustable ring,ch 1, 6 sc in ring, place marker, sl st in first sc: 6 sc

Round 2: ch 1, 2 sc in each sc around, sl st in first sc: 12 sc

Round 3: ch 1, (sc in next sc, 2 sc in next sc) around, sl st in first sc: 18 sc

Round 4: ch 1, (2 sc in next sc, sc in next 2 sc) around, sl st in first sc: 24 sc

Round 5-7: ch 2, hdc in each st around, sl st in first hdc: 24 hdc

Round 8: ch 3, dc in each hdc around, sl st in first dc: 24 dc

Finish off.

August 6 Seashore Dishcloth

Materials:

Super Fine Weight Yarn (approximately 40 yards of each)

Crochet hook F (3.75mm)

Instructions

Row 1: ch 38, sc in second ch from hook, *skip next 2 ch, 5 dc in next ch, skip next 2 ch, sc in next ch, repeat from * across: 37 sts

Row 2: ch 3, turn, 2 dc in first sc, skip 2 dc, sc in next dc, *skip next 2 dc, 5 dc in next sc, skip next 2 dc, sc in next dc, repeat from * across until 3 sts remains, skip 2 dc, 3 dc in last sc: 37 sts

Row 3: ch 1, turn, sc in first dc, *skip 2 dc, 5 dc in next sc, skip 2 dc, sc in next dc, repeat from * across: 37 sts

Row 4 – 25: repeat Rows 2 – 3

Do not finish off, continue with border.

August 7 Talia Earrings

Materials:

Size 10 thread (approximately 10 yards)

Crochet Hook C (2.75 mm)

Earwires   crochet yarn size 0

Instructions

Round 1: make adjustable ring, ch 1, (2 sc, ch 1) 2 times in ring, sl st in first sc: 6 sts

Round 2: ch 1, turn, 2 sc in each st around, sl st in first sc: 12 sc

Round 3: ch 1, turn, *(2sc in next sc, sc in next sc) 2 times, 2 sc in next sc, ch 1, skip 1 sc, repeat from * 1 more time, sl st in first sc: 18 sts

Round 4-5: ch 1, turn, sc in each sc around, sl st in first sc: 18 sc

Finish off and block. Attach to earwires.

August 8 Pop Out Flower

Materials:

Light Weight Yarn (approximately 10 yards)

Crochet Hook F (3.75 mm)   crochet yarn size 3

Instructions

Round 1: make adjustable ring, ch 1, 6 sc in ring, sl st in first sc: 6 sc

Round 2: ch 1, 2 sc in each sc around, sl st in first sc: 12 sc

Round 3: ch 1, (sc in next sc, 2 sc in next sc) around, sl st in first sc: 18 sc

Round 4: ch 1, sc in each sc around, sl st in first sc: 18 sc

Round 5: ch 1, 2 sc in each sc around, sl st in first sc: 36 sc

Round 6: ch 15, skip 5 sc, sl st in next sc, (sl st in next sc, ch 15, skip 4 sc, sl st in next sc) around: 101 sts

Round 7: ch 1, (8 sc, ch 3, 8 sc) in each ch-space around, sl st in first sc: 114 sts

Finish off.

August 9 Peek-a-Boo Mug Cozy

Materials:

Medium Weight Yarn (approximately 30 yards)

Crochet Hook I (5.50 mm)   crochet yarn size 4

Instructions

Row 1: ch 10, sc in second ch from hook and in each ch across, turn: 9 sc

Row 2: ch 3, dc in each sc across, turn: 9 dc

Row 3: ch 3, dtr in each dc across: 9 dtr

Finish off.

Row 1: ch 29, sc in second ch from hook and in each ch across, turn: 28 sc

Row 2: sl st in first sc, dc in next 26 dc, turn: 26 dc

Row 3: ch 1, sc in each dc across, turn: 26 sc

Row 4: ch 5, dtr in first 4 sc, ch 8, sk 8 sc, dtr in rem sc, turn: 26 sts

Row 5: ch 1, sc in each st across, turn: 26 sc

Row 6: ch 3, dc in each sc across, turn: 26 sts

Ros 7, ch 2, sc in second ch from hook and in each st across, fsc at end of row: 28 sc

Finish off and sew the ends of the short sides together.

August 10 iPod Cozy

Materials:

Medium Weight Yarn (approximately 7 yards)

Crochet Hook G (4.00 mm)   crochet yarn size 4

Instructions

Round 1: ch 14, sl st into first ch made to form a ring, sc into each ch around: 13 sc

Round 2 – 6: sc into each sc around: 13 sc

Finish off by slip stitching the ends together. Break off and weave in ends

August 11 Thick Pot Handle Cozy

Materials:

Medium Weight Yarn (small amount of blue and yellow)

Crochet Hook J (6.00 mm)   crochet yarn size 4

Instructions

Round 1: with 2 strands of yarn held together (one blue and one yellow) ch 5, sl st in first ch made forming a loop, 10 hdc in loop, place marker: 10 hdc

Round 2 – 10: hdc in each hdc around: 10 hdc

Round 11: hdc in each hdc around, sl st in next hdc, finish off: 10 hdc

August 12 Chapstick Keychain Cozy

Materials:

Medium Weight Yarn (small amount of main color)

Crochet Hook H (5.00 mm)   crochet yarn size 4

Instructions

Round 1: ch 3, 8 hdc in third ch from hook, sl st in top of beginning ch-3: 8 hdc

Round 2 : ch 2, hdc in each hdc around, sl st in top of beginning ch-2: 8 hdc

Repeat round 2, 7 times or until the cozy covers your chapstick.

Round 3: ch 8, skip 4 hdc, sc in next hdc, finish off

August 13 Slouchy Beanie

Materials

8mm hook

Chunky wool

Instructions

Rnd 1: Ch 4, dc into the 4th ch from the hook and ch 1, in the same chain space *dc + ch 1* 6 more times (8) Join with first ch with a sl st.

Rnd 2: Ch 4, *1 dc + chain 1* twice in each chain space (16) Join with the first ch with a sl st.

Rnd 3: Ch 4, *1 dc + ch 1* twice in first chain space, *1 dc + ch1 in next dc, 1 dc + ch 1 twice in next dc* repeat to end of Rnd (24) join with the first ch with a sl st.

Rnd 4 - 12: Ch 4, 1 dc + ch 1 in each chain space, join with sl st (24

Rnd 13: Ch 1, 2 sc in each chain space, join with first ch with a sl st (48)

Rnd 14: Ch 1, 1 sc in each sc all the way around, join with sl st (48)

Fasten off and weave in ends.

August 14 Open Tunisian Scarf

Materials

Fine Weight Yarn (approximately 75 yards)

Tunisian crochet Hook H (5.00 mm) crochet yarn size 2

Instructions

Row 1: ch 22, pull up a loop in second ch from hook and in each ch across, work return pass: 21 tss

Row 2: ch 2, (tdc in next 6 sts, yo 4 times, skip 4 sts) until 1 st remains, tdc in last st: 21 sts

Row 3: ch 2, tdc in first st, (yo 4 times, skip 4 sts, tdc in next 6 sts) across: 21 sts

Row 4-69: repeat rows 2-3

Row 70: sl st in each st across: 21 sl st

Finish off.

August 15 Spring Choker

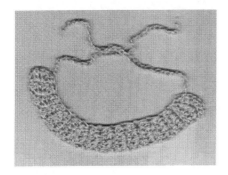

Materials

Yarn size 3

"F" Crochet hook.

Instructions

Round 1: Ch 40. Sc in second ch from hook, and in next 5 chains (6 sc total.)

Ch 6 and turn. Sl st into 12th ch from hook (the 1st of the just crocheted 6 sc.)

Round 2: Ch 3 and turn. ***Dc four times around the "6 sc ch bar." Sl st to the last st on the "ch 6 bar" you are working on.

Round 3: Ch 6, turn. Sl st to 12th chain from hook. Ch 3 and turn.

Round 4:- Repeat from *** for a total of 16 group/sections.

At end of 16th group/section, instead of chain 3, chain 35. Tie off.

Tie a little knot at the end of each of your "tie" chains to help prevent fraying.

August 16 Badge Holder

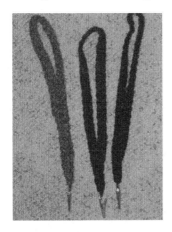

Materials:

Crown yarn

G hook

Instructions

Row 1: With yarn and G hook ch-3, hdc 2nd ch from hook, hdc next ch, ch-1, turn. (2 sts)

Row 2: Hdc every st across, ch-1, turn.

Rep row 2 until piece will fit easily over your head, do not fasten off.

Place ends of piece tog and working through both thickness, hdc ea st across, ch-1, turn. (2 sts)

Rep row 2, twice.

Next row: hdc dec 2 sts tog as 1, ch-1, turn.

Next row: hdc only st, fasten off.

Place the single st in the end of the clip, with pliers, press ea side of the clip down to cover st.

August 17 Cat Scrubbie

Materials:

Medium Weight Yarn (approximately 15 yards)

Scrap yarn for eyes and face

Crochet Hook J (6.0 mm)

Instructions

Row 1: Ch 12, dc in 4th ch from hook, 2 dc in next ch, dc in next 5 ch, 2 dc in next ch, dc in last ch, turn: 11 dc

Row 2: Ch 3, dc in first dc, 2 dc in next dc, dc in next 7 dc, 2 dc in next dc, dc in last dc, turn: 13 dc

Row 3: Ch 3, dc in first dc, dc2tog, dc in next 7 dc, dc2tog, dc in last dc, turn : 11 dc

Rows 4 – 6: Ch 3, dc in each dc across, turn

Row 7: Ch 4, tr3tog, finish off.

Attach yarn to beginning of row 6, ch 4, tr3tog, finish off.

Using photo as a guide embroider face to scrubbie.

August 18 Cat Ear Headband

Materials:

Cloth Covered Headband

Bulky Eyelash Yarn (approximately 25 yards)

Crochet Hook H (5 mm)

Scissors

Super Glue

crochet yarn size 6

Instructions

Row 1: For a child's headband sc 54 times over the head-band. I recommend leaving about 1 1/2″ of each end of the headband uncovered so it's more comfortable to wear. Weave in loose ends.

Ear

Row 1: To create an ear, count 16 sc from the edge of the headband, sl st to join in the 16th sc, sc in next 7 sc: 7 sc

Row 2-3: ch 1, turn, sc in next 7 sc: 7 sc

Row 4-8: ch 1, turn, skip first sc, sc in next sc and in each sc across

Finish off. Repeat ear instructions on the other side of the headband for the second ear

August 19 Cat Toy

Materials:

Medium Weight Yarn

Crochet Hook

Scissors

Instructions

Row 1: holding crochet hook upside down, wrap 20 times around bottom of hook: 20 wrap

Row 2: overlapping previous row and working in opposite direction, wrap 20 times: 20 wrap

Repeat row 2, until your work looks like a ball

Row 3: slide work off of hook and turn 90 degrees, wrap 20 times: 20 wrap

Repeat row 3, until toy is as large as you desire, then finish off.

August 20 Miss Mouse Cat Trip Toy

Materials:

Grey Medium Weight Eyelash Yarn

Pink Medium Weight Eyelash Yarn

Crochet Hook I (5.5 mm)

Curved Upholstery needle

Catnip (1/4 cup)

Instructions

Row 1: with grey, ch 3, sc in second ch from hook 2 sc in next ch, ch 1, turn: 3 sc

Row 2-9: sc in each sc across until 1 sc remains, 2 sc in last sc, ch 1, turn.

Row 10-11: sc in each sc across, ch 1, turn: 9 sc

Row 12- 19: skip first sc, sc in next sc and in each sc across, ch 1, turn.

Finish off.

August 21 No-Sew Pencil Skirt

Materials:

Fingering Weight Yarn (approximately 15 yards)

Crochet Hook E (3.50 mm)

1 ft of fingering weight yarn or 5 in. of elastic cord crochet yarn size 4

Instructions

Round 1: ch 25, sl st in first ch to form ring, ch 2, hdc in each ch around, sl st in first hdc: 25 hdc

Round 2-4: ch 3, dc in each st around, sl st in first dc

Round 5: ch 3, (dc in next 4 dc, 2 dc in next dc) around, sl st in first dc: 30 dc

Round 6: ch 3, dc in each st around, sl st in first dc: 30 dc

Round 7: ch 3, (dc in next 5 dc, dc2tog) around, sl st in first dc: 25 dc

Round 8: ch 3, (dc2tog, dc in next 3 dc) around, sl st in first dc: 20 dc

Finish off.

August 22 Lemon Cake Cozy

Materials

H/8 (5.00MM) hook

Red Heart Worsted Medium weight yarn in cornmeal, white and chocolate

Instructions

ch16

1 skip 1 ch, 15 sc across

2-6 ch 1 turn 15 sc across

7 ch 1 turn. sc in next 2 sc, ch 11, skip 11sc, sc in last 2 sc

8-15 ch 1 turn. 15 sc across

Leave long tail for sewing and break off.

Icing sides (for corner peice you will need 2)

(Yellow) Ch 16

1 skip 1 ch, 15 sc across

2-19 ch 1, 15 sc across.

Break off with long tail and secure.

August 23: Craft Bangles

Materials:

Super Fine Weight yarn

Crochet Hook F (3.75 mm)

3 1/4" craft band

25 seed beads

Instructions

Row 1: string 25 beads onto the yarn.

Make a slip knot to the front of the band

Pull up a lp and ch 1 over ring, *6 sc into ring,

Pull a bead up close to the hook, ch 1 with bead

Push the bead up to make sure it is visible, repeat from * until you have used all the beads or the band is wrapped as tightly as desired,

sl st to beginning sc: 150 sc

Finish off.

August 24 French Press Cozy Pattern

Materials

Yarn:

1 skein [100% cotton; 120 yards; 70.9 grams; worsted weight]

Crochet Hook:

US H/5mm hook

2 small toggle buttons

Tapestry needle

Ch 16 sts loosely.

Instruction

Foundation Row: Sc in 2nd ch from hook, *ch 1, sk next ch, 1 sc in next ch; rep from * 7 times.

Mock Weave: Ch 1, sk 1st sc, *1 sc in next ch-1 sp, ch 1, sk next sc st; rep from * 7 times, sc in turning ch of previous row.

*Rep Mock Weave row until piece measures 8.25" or desired length from beginning.

Button Loops

Row 1: Ch 1, sk 1st sc, *sc in next ch-1 sp, sc in next sc; rep from * 7 times -- 14 sc.

Row 2: Sl st in first 2 sc, ch 3, sk next sc, sl st in next 7 sc, ch 3, sk next sc, sl st in last 2 sc.

Fasten off and weave in ends.

Sew buttons to beginning edge to correspond to button loops made on last row.

August 25 Water Bottle Cozy

Materials

Yarn:

Lily Sugar'n Cream [100% cotton; 120 yards; 70.9 grams; worsted weight]

Main Color: 1 skein Stonewash,

Alternate color 1 skein

Crochet Hook:

US G/4.5mm crochet hook

Tapestry needle

Instructions

Foundation Row: Dc in 4th ch from hook, dc in each ch to end -- 23 dc + turning ch.

Row 1: Ch 3 (counts as 1st dc), sk first dc, fp dc around next 22 sts, dc in turning ch of previous row -- 24 sts.

Row 2: Ch 3 (counts as 1st dc), sk first dc, bp dc around next 22 sts, dc in turning ch of previous row -- 24 sts.

*Rep Rows 1 and 2 until piece measures 8.5" from beginning, or desired length (circumference of your water bottle).

Fasten off and weave in ends.

August 26 Soap Holder

Materials

Yarn:

1 skein Knit Picks Cotlin [70% Tanguis Cotton / 30% Linen; 50 grams; 123 yards; DK weight], Color "nightfall"

Instructions

Rows 1-3: Ch 1, sc in each st across -- 18 sc.

Row 4: Ch 5, sk next st, sc in next st, *ch 2, sk 2 sts, dc in next st, ch 2, sk 2 sts, sc in next st; rep from * once more, ch 2, sk 2 sts, dc.

Row 5: Ch 3, dc in next sc, *ch 2, sc in next dc, ch 2, dc in next sc; rep from * once more, ch 2, sc in 3rd loop of turning ch.

Row 6: Ch 5, sc in next dc, *ch 2, dc in next sc, ch 2, sc in next dc; rep from * once more, ch 2, dc in 2nd loop of turning ch.

Row 7: Ch 3, dc in next sc, *ch 2, sc in next dc, ch 2, dc in next sc; rep from * once more, ch 2, sc in 3rd loop of turning ch.

Rows 8-15: Repeat Rows 6 and 7 another 4 times.

Row 16: Repeat Row 6 once more.

Rows 17: Ch 1, sc in each st and ch across -- 18 sts.

Rows 18-19: Ch 1, sc in each st across -- 18 sts.

Fasten off.

August 27 Leaf Cozy

Materials

Radiant Yellow Yarn

Hook: H

Instructions

Ch 34, join with a sl st.

Rnd 1: Sc around. (34)

Rnd 2: Sc around. Join and change color to Fern with a sl st. (34)

Rnd 3: Sc around. Join and change color to Raspberry with a sl st into back loop of first st made in this Rnd. (34)

Rnd 4: Work in back loops only. Sc around. (34)

Rnd 5-8: Work in both loops. Sc around. (34)

Rnd 9: Work in both loops. Sc around. Join and change color to Fern with a sl st. (34)

Rnd 10: Sc around. Join and change color to Radiant Yellow with a sl st into back loop of first st made in this Rnd. (34)

Rnd11: Work in back loops only. Sc around. (34)

Rnd 12: Work in both loops. Sc around. (34)

Sl St. Finish off and weave in ends.

Insert twig under any st of Rnd 9.

August 28 Brown Cozy

Materials

H hook

Brown cotton

Instructions

Make an adjustable loop.

Rnd 1: 6 sc in loop, pull loop taut. (6sc)

Rnd 2: 2 sc in each st around. (12sc)

Rnd 3: (sc in next st, 2 sc in next st) repeat around. (18sc)

Rnd 4: (sc in next 2 sts, 2 sc in next st) repeat around. (24sc)

Rnd 5: (sc in next 3 sts, 2 sc in next st) repeat around. (30sc)

Rnds 6-24: sc in each st around, sl st in next st at end of rnd 24 (30sc each rnd).

Rnd 25: rev sc around, fasten off and weave in ends.

August 29 Detachable Monkey Ears

Materials

1.5 oz brown worsted weight cotton

Small amount tan worsted weight cotton

Small amount black embroidery floss or yarn

H hook

F hook

2 buttons

tapestry needle

Instructions

With F hook and brown cotton, ch 2.

Row 1: 6sc in 2nd ch from hook, ch 1, turn. (6sc)

Row 2: 2 sc in each st across, fasten off leaving long tail for sewing. (12sc)

August 30 Cotton Sleeve

Materials

Medium cotton yarn

4 mm crochet hook

Instructions

Chain 35 and join first and last sts to form a ring, being careful not to twist sts.

Round 1-2: Sc 35 (35 sts)

Round 3: *Sc 5, dec 1*, rep 5 times (30 sts)

Round 4: Sc 30 (30 sts)

Round 5: *Sc 4, dec 1*, rep 5 times (25 sts)

Round 6-9: Sc 25

Fasten off and weave in end.

August 31 Hemp Sleeve

Materials

Hemp

4 mm crochet hook

Chain 30 and join first and last sts to form a ring, being careful not to twist sts.

Round 1-2: Sc 30 (30 sts)

Round 3: *Sc 4, dec 1*, rep 5 times (25 sts)

Round 4: Sc 25 (25 sts)

Round 5: *Sc 3, dec 1*, rep 5 times (20 sts)

Round 6: Sc 20

Fasten off and weave in end.

September

September 1: Comfortable Mug Cozy

Materials:

Red Heart, 3-ply acrylic yarn, 1 skein multicolor and contrasting color

Crochet hook size 4mm.

2 buttons

Yarn needle

Instructions

Rnd 1: Ch 4 (Note: beginning ch 3 counts as 1st dc), 11 dc in 4th ch from hook, join with sl st on top of beg ch 3. (12 dc)

Rnd 2: Ch 3, 2 dc in each dc around, join. (23 dc)

Rnd 3: Ch 3, 2 dc in each dc around, join. (46 dc)

Rnd 4: Ch 2 (counts as hdc), hdc in each dc around, join on top of beg ch 2. (46 hdc)

Continue to work on the body of cozy, this time working in rows. Turn, this becomes the right side.

Row 1: Ch 2 (counts as hdc), (hdc in the next 7 st, 2 hdc in next st), 4 times, hdc in next 9 sts, leave the last 4 sts unworked, turn. (46 hdc)

Row 2: Ch 2, hdc in each hdc across, turn. (46 hdc)

Rows 3-5: repeat row 2. At the end of row 5, don't turn , ch 10, sc on the side of row 3, turn and sl st back on each ch just made, sl st on top of last hdc of row 5.

Row 6: repeat row 2

Rows 7-8: repeat row 2. (Note: change color at the end of row 8)

Row 9: With contrasting color, repeat row 2, ch 15, and sl st on top of last hdc of this row.

Row 10: (edging) Ch 1, sc in same st, sc in each st across. Fasten off.

Finishing: Sew two buttons near the edge of rows opposite the two button loops. Weave in ends.

September 2: Monster Apple Crochet Cozy

Materials

Worsted weight cotton yarn

White yarn

Black crochet thread

Color for the hair

H hook, D hook

One 5/8 in. button

a small piece of felt for the tooth

Tapestry needle

Scissors

Instructions

With main color, make a magic ring.

Round 1: Ch 1 (does not count as st here and throughout), work 6 sc in ring, join — 6 sts.

Round 2: Ch 1, work 2 sc in same st as join and in each st around, join — 12 sts.

Round 3: Ch 1, work 2 sc in same st as join, 1 sc in next, *2 sc in next, 1 sc in next, rep from * around, join — 18 sts.

Round 4: Ch 1, work 2 sc in same st as join, 1 sc in each of the next 2 sts, *2 sc in next st, 1 sc in each of the next 2 sts, rep from * around, join — 24 sts.

Rounds 5 through 11: Ch 1, work 1 sc in same st as join and each st around, join — 24 sts.

Fasten off, leaving a tail of approx. 6 in.

September 3: French Mug Cozy

Materials:

Cotton yarn

Size H8 - 5 mm crochet hook

Button that is 1" in diameter

Needle

Instructions

Rnd 1: 6 sc into an adjustable ring and pull the ring closed (6).

Rnd 2: 2 sc in each sc around (12).

Rnd 3: [Sc in next sc, 2 sc in next sc] 6 times (18).

Rnd 4: [Sc in next 2 sc, 2 sc in next sc] 6 times (24).

Rnd 5: [Sc in next 3 sc, 2 sc in next sc] 6 times (30).

Rnd 6: [Sc in next 4 sc, 2 sc in next sc] 6 times (36).

Rnd 7: working in back loops only, sc in each sc around (36).

Rnd 8: sc in each sc around (36).

Now you are going to work in rows.

Row 9: ch 1, turn, sc in next 32 sc, ch 1, turn (32).

Rows 10-19: sc in each sc across, ch 1, turn (32).

Continue to sc evenly along the opening for the handle until to reach the top of Row 19 on the other side of the opening. Ch 18 (this forms the loop that goes around the button).

Row 20: Continue to sc in first sc on Row 19 and sc in each sc across (32).

Finish off and weave in ends.

Sew the button.

September 4: iPod Crochet Pattern

Materials

Worsted weight yarn in 2 colors,

Size H crochet hook

Instructions

Chain 11

Row 1: hdc in second chain from hook, hdc in each chain (9 hdc). Hdc twice in last chain and then hdc along the back side of the chain. Join to first hdc with a slip stitch.

Row 2-5: hdc in each stitch around, joining rounds each time with a slip stitch.

Row 6: Chain 4, tr in each stitch around. Join with a slip stitch.

Row 7: Chain 1, sc in each stitch around. Join with a slip stitch.

Row 8-9: Chain 2, hdc in each stitch around. Join with a slip stitch.

Row 10: Chain 3, dc in each stitch around. Join with a slip stitch.

Row 11: Chain 2, hdc in each stitch around. Join with a slip stitch.

Row 12: Chain 1, sc in each stitch around. Join with a slip stitch. Finish off.

Row 13: Join second color to any of the stitches. Chain 4 and then single crochet to the same stitch as your join. Slip stitch into first stitch and finish off.

Weave in all ends.

September 5: Mayflower Necklace

Materials:

Lace Weight Yarn (approximately 16 yards)

Crochet hook 6 (1.80 mm)

Necklace

8 Jump rings

Instructions

Flower

Round 1: make an adjustable ring, (ch 2, 2 dc, ch 2, sl st) 4 times in ring: 8 dc

Finish off.

Attach one jump ring to each flower and then attach to one link every 1/2" on necklace chain.

September 6: Tiara Headband

Materials:

Fine Weight Yarn (approximately 15 yards)

Crochet hook E (3.50 mm)

Instructions

Row 1: ch 86, sc in second ch from hook and each ch across: 85 sc

Row 2: ch 1, turn, sc in firs sc, *ch 5, skip next 3 sc, sc in next sc, repeat from * across: 21 ch-5 spaces

Row 3: ch 1, turn, (3 sc, ch 4, sl st in last sc made, 2 sc) in each ch-5 space across, work last sc in last sc: 105 sc

Finish off.

Cut 2 strands of yarn measuring 16" and attach 1 strand at both ends.

September 7: Summer Waves Crochet Placemat Pattern

Materials

Cotton Yarn

Crochet hook 6 (1.80 mm)

Instruction

Ch 58 loosely.

Row 1: Sc in the second ch from hook. *Sc in next st, then hdc in next 2 sts, dc in next 2 sts, tr in next 3 sts, dc in next 2 sts, hdc in next 2 sts, sc in next 2 sts. Repeat from * to end of row. (57 sts)

Row 2: Ch1 and turn. Sc in ea st across to end. (57 sc)

Row 3: With Color B, ch 4 and turn. Work this row and all remaining odd numbered rows in BLO, except for the very last st of the row. *Tr in next st, dc in next 2 sts, hdc in next

2 sts, sc in next 3 sts, hdc in next 2 sts, dc in next 2 sts, tr in next 2 sts. Repeat from * to end of row. (57 sts)

Row 4: Ch1 and turn. Sc in ea st across to end. (57 sc)

Rows 5 – 30: Repeat Rows 1 – 4 6x, and then repeat Rows 1 – 2 once more. Use Color C for Rows 23 – 24 if desired. Break yarn and finish off.

September 8: Summer Waves Crochet Coaster Pattern

Materials

Cotton Yarn

Crochet hook 6 (1.80 mm)

Instruction

Ch 16 loosely.

Row 1: Sc in the second ch from hook. Sc in next st, then hdc in next 2 sts, dc in next 2 sts, tr in next 3 sts, dc in next 2 sts, hdc in next 2 sts, sc in next 2 sts. (15 sts)

Row 2: Ch1 and turn. Sc in ea st across to end. (15 sc)

Row 3: With Color B, ch 4 and turn. Work this row and all remaining odd numbered rows in BLO, except for the very last st of the row. Tr in next st, dc in next 2 sts, hdc in next 2 sts, sc in next 3 sts, hdc in next 2 sts, dc in next 2 sts, tr in next 2 sts. (15 sts)

Row 4: Ch1 and turn. Sc in ea st across to end. (15 sc)

Rows 5 – 6: Repeat Rows 1 – 2.

Rows 7 – 8: With Color C, repeat Rows 3 – 4.

Rows 9 – 10: Repeat Rows 1 – 2.

September 9: Crochet Placemat

Materials

Yarn Cotton Classic

Hook; US 6/G/4.00 mm

Instructions

Row 1: Ch 91, turn, sc in the second ch from the hook and in each remaining ch across. (90 sc)

Row 2: Turn, ch 1, sc in each sc across.

Repeat row 2: Until the color pattern has been completed 16 times, then make alternating rows

Clip yarn and weave in ends.

Color Pattern:

Row 1: Color A

Row 2: Color B

Rows 3~5: Color C

September 10: Lace Flower

Materials:

Fine Weight Yarn

Crochet Hook G (4.25 mm)   crochet yarn size 2

Instructions

Round 1: ch 6, sl st in first ch made, ch 1, 3 sc in each ch around, sl st in first sc: 15 sc

Round 2: ch 3, (dc in next 3 sc, ch 1) around, sl st in first dc: 20 sts

Round 3: ch 2 (hdc in next dc, 2 hdc in next dc, hdc in next dc, ch 2) around, sl st in first hdc: 30 sts

Round 4: ch 3, (dc2tog 2 times, ch 7) around, sl st in first dc: 45 sts

Round 5: ch 1, (sc in next 5 sts, 2 sc in next st, sc in next 3 sts) around, sl st in first sc: 50 sc

Finish off.

September 11: Puffy Flower Coaster

Materials:

Super Fine Weight Yarn (approximately 5 yards)

Crochet Hook B (2.25 mm)   crochet yarn size 1

Instructions

Round 1: make adjustable ring, 6 sc in ring, sl st in first sc: 6 sc

Round 2: ch 1, (2 sc in next sc, sc in next sc) around: 9 sc

Round 3: ch 1, (sc in next 2 sc, 2 sc in next sc) around: 12 sc

Round 4: (ch 4, bobble in next sc, ch 4, sl st in next sc) around: 6 bobbles

Row 5: ch 61, 3 sc in second ch from hook: 3 sc

Row 6: ch 1, turn, 2 sc in each sc across: 6 sc

Row 7: ch 1, turn, (2 sc in next sc, sc in next sc) across: 9 sc

Finish off

September 12: Shell Bracelet

Materials:

Light Fingering Weight Yarn (approximately 25 yards)

Crochet Hook E (3.50 mm)

6 mm Bead   crochet yarn size 1

Instructions

Round 1: ch 37, 3 sc in second ch from hook ch, sc in next 33 ch, 3 sc in last ch, working in bottom/opposite side of the chain, 3 sc in next ch, sc in next 33 ch, 3 sc in last ch, sl st in first sc: 78 sc

Round 2: ch 3, 3 dc in first sc, sc in next sc, skip 2 sc, 5 dc in next sc, (skip 4 sc, 5 dc in next sc) 6 times, skip 2 sc, dc in next sc, 3 dc in each of next 2 sc, sc in next sc, skip 2 sc, 5 dc in next sc, (skip 4 sc, 5 dc in next sc) 6 times, skip 2 sc, dc in next sc, 3 dc in last sc, (sl st, ch 3, sl st) in first dc: 84 dc

Finish off. Sew bead to the end of the bracelet on the right side opposite the loop.

September 13: Easy Pen Case

Materials:

Light Weight Yarn (approximately 35 yards of each color)

Crochet Hook J (6.00 mm)   crochet yarn size 3

Instructions

Round 1: holding 3 strands of yarn together, ch 5, sc in back loop of second ch from hook and each ch across, working on opposite side of chain, sc in front loop in each ch across, sl st in first sc: 8 sc

Round 2: ch 3, dc in each sc around, sl st in first dc: 8 dc

Round 3-10: ch 3, dc in each dc around, sl st in first dc: 8 dc

To finish off, cut a long tail and pull through last remaining loop. Knot end of tail then weave through the top of each dc around. This makes the drawstring.

September 14: Sparkly Crescent

Materials:

Fine Weight Yarn (approximately 2 yards)

2 beads (any size the yarn can fit through)

Crochet Hook B (2.25 mm)   crochet yarn size 2

Instructions

Row 1: ch 1 with bead, ch 7, ch 1 with bead, sl st in first ch from hook, sc in next 2 ch, 3 hdc in next ch, 2 dc in next ch, 2 hdc in next ch, sc in next 2 ch, sl st in last ch: 12 sts

Row 2: turn, sl st in first 2 sts, sc in next 3 sts, hdc in next 2 sts, sc in next 3 sts, sl st in next 2 sts: 12 sts

Finish off.

September 15: Classic Square Coaster

Materials:

Medium Weight Yarn (approximately 20 yards per coaster)

Crochet Hook H (5.00 mm)   crochet yarn size 4

Instructions

Round 1: ch 3, 12 dc in third ch from hook, sl st in first dc: 12 dc

Round 2: ch 2, (4 dc in next dc, dc in next 2 dc) around, sl st in first dc: 24 dc

Round 3: ch 2, dc in first 2 dc, (4 dc in next dc, dc in next 5 dc) 3 times, 4 dc in next dc, dc in last 3 dc, sl st in first dc: 36 dc

Round 4: ch 2, dc in first 4 dc, (4 dc in next dc, dc in next 8 dc) 3 times, 4 dc in next dc, dc in last 4 dc, sl st in first dc: 48 dc

Finish off.

September 16: Tunisian Heart Coaster

Materials:

Medium Weight Yarn (approximately 10 yards)

Tunisian Crochet Hook J (6.00 mm) crochet yarn size 4

Instructions

Row 1: Forward pass: ch 16, pull up a loop in second ch from hook and each ch across, work return pass: 15 tss

Rows 2-4: tss in each st across: 15 tss

Row 5: tss in first 7 tss, yo, skip 1 st, tss in last 7 tss: 15 sts

Row 6: tss in first 6 tss, yo, skip 1 st, tss in next st, yo, skip 1 st, tss in last 6 tss: 15 sts

Row 7: tss in first 5 tss, yo, skip 1 st, tss in next 3 sts, yo, skip 1 st, tss in last 5 tss: 15 sts

Row 8-9: tss in first 4 tss, yo, skip 1 st, tss in next 5 sts, yo, skip 1 st, tss in last 4 tss: 15 sts

Row 10: tss in first 4 tss, yo, skip 1 st, tss in next 2 tss, yo, skip 1 st, tss in next 2 tss, yo, skip 1 st, tss in last 4 tss: 15 sts

Row 11: tss in first 5 tss, yo, skip 1 st, 3 tss in next tss, yo, skip 1 st, tss in last 5 tss: 15 sts

Rows 12-13: tss in each st across: 15 sts

Use single crochet Tunisian finish.

September 17: Square Coaster

Materials:

Medium Weight Yarn (approximately 25 yards of each color)

Crochet Hook H (5.00 mm)   crochet yarn size 4

Instructions

Round 1: make adjustable ring, ch 1, 6 sc in ring, sl st in first sc: 6 sc

Round 2: ch, 2 hdc in each sc around, sl st in first hdc: 12 hdc

Round 3: ch 4 (counts as 1 dc and 1 ch), skip first 2 hdc, 3 dc in next hdc, dc in next hdc, (ch 1, skip 1 hdc, 3 dc in next hdc, dc in next hdc) 2 times, ch 1, skip 1 hdc, 3 dc in next hdc, sl st in third ch of beginning ch-4: 20 sts

Round 4: ch 1, sc in next 3 sts, 3 sc in next dc, (sc in next 4 sts, 3 sc in next dc) 3 times, sc in last dc, sl st in first sc: 28 sc

Round 5: ch 2, dc in next 4 sc, 3 dc in next sc, (dc in next 6 sc, 3 dc in next sc) 3 times, dc in last 2 sc, sl st in first dc: 36 sc

Finish off

September 18: Spoked Coaster

Materials:

Medium Weight Yarn (approximately 10 yards)

Crochet Hook H (5.00 mm)   crochet yarn size 4

Instructions

Round 1: make adjustable ring, ch 1, 6 sc in ring, sl st in first sc: 6 sc

Round 2: ch 2, (hdc, fphdc) in each sc around, sl st in first hdc: 12 sc

Round 3: ch 2, (2 hdc in next hdc, fphdc in next hdc) around, sl st in first hdc: 18 sc

Round 4: ch 2, (hdc in next hdc, 2 hdc in next hdc, fphdc in next hdc) around, sl st in first hdc: 24 hdc

Round 5: ch 2, (2 hdc in next hdc, hdc in next hdc, 2 hdc in next hdc, fphdc in next hdc) around, sl st in first hdc: 36 hdc

Finish off.

September 19: Stem Glass Scarf

Materials:

Medium Weight Yarn (approximately 15 yards)

Crochet Hook F (3.75 mm)   crochet yarn size 4

Instructions

Row 1: ch 42, sc in second chain from hook and in each ch across: 41 sc

Row 2: ch 1, turn, sc in each ch across: 41 sc

Finish off.

September 20: Crayon Link Scarf

Materials:

Medium Weight Yarn (approximately 20 yards of each color/8 colors/3 links per color)

Crochet Hook G (4.00 mm)

Yarn Needle   crochet yarn size 4

Instructions

Link: (make 24 links, 3 in each of the 8 colors)

Round 1: with main color, ch 40, sl st in first ch to form a ring: 40 ch

Round 2: hdc in each ch around: 40 hdc

Round 3 – hdc in each hdc around: 40 hdc

Finish off. For each link after the first link, loop chain on round 1 through previous link before making the slip stitch.

September 21: Mimosa Scarf

Materials:

Chunky Weight Yarn (approximately 80 yards)

Crochet Hook M (9.00 mm)

Yarn Needle

Instructions

Row 1: sc in 25th ch from hook, *ch 12, skip 9 sts, sc in next st, repeat from * across: 15 loops

Row 2: ch 6, sc in middle of first loop, * ch 12, sc in middle of next loop, repeat from * across, ch 6, sc at end of last loop: 16 loops

Row 3: ch 12, skip first loop, sc in middle of next loop, * ch 12, sc in middle of next loop, repeat from * across: 15 loops

Rows 4-5: repeat row 2 and 3

Row 6: repeat row 2

Row 7: ch 10, skip first loop, sc in middle of next loop, * ch 10, sc in middle of next loop, repeat from * across: 15 loops

Finish off.

September 22: Knot Stitch Shawl

Materials:

Medium Weight Yarn (approximately 200 yards)

Crochet Hook I (5.5 mm)   crochet yarn size 4

Instructions

Start by making a chain of 36 knots or as many knots to form the desired width of the shawl

Row 1: make 2 knots, sl st in third knot from hook, (make 2 knots, sl st in next knot) across: 72 knots, 36 sl sts

Row 2: make 1 knot, turn, sl st in first knot, (make 2 knots, skip 1 knot, sl st in next knot) across: 71 knots, 35 sl sts

Repeat row 2 ten times or until shawl is the height that you want it. Note that for each row you do, there is 1 less knot and 1 less sl st than the previous row.

September 23: Keychain Card Holder

Materials:

Sport Weight Yarn (approximately 5 yards)

Crochet Hook E (3.50 mm)   crochet yarn size 2

Instructions

Round 1: ch 7, sc in second ch from hook and each ch across, working on opposite side of ch, sc in each ch across: 12 sc

Round 2 – 5: ch 3, dc in each st around, sl st in first dc: 12 dc

Finish off.

September 24: Lip Balm Holder

Materials:

Medium Weight Yarn (approximately 10 yards)

Crochet Hook I (5.50 mm)

Instructions

Round 1: Make an adjustable ring, ch 3, 8 dc in ring, sl st in top of beg ch-3: 8 dc

Rounds 2-8:ch 3, dc in each dc, sl st in top of beg ch-3: 8 dc

Finish off.

September 25: Watermelon Potholder

Materials:

Red Worsted Weight Yarn

Green Worsted Weight Yarn

Black Worsted Weight Yarn

Crochet Hook H (5 mm)

Yarn Needle

Scissors

crochet yarn size 4

Instructions

Round 1: with red, ch 4, sl st in first ch made to form a ring, ch 1, working in back loops only now and throughout, 2 sc in each ch around: 8 sc

Round 2-3: ch 1, 2 sc in each sc around, sl st in top of beginning ch-1

Round 4: sc in each sc around, sl st in top of beginning ch-1: 32 sc

Round 5: ch 1, 2 sc in each sc around, sl st in top of beginning ch-1: 64 sc

Round 6: sc in each sc around, sl st in top of beginning ch-1: 64 sc

Finish off.

Round 7-8: with green, sl st to join, ch 1, sc in each sc around, sl st in top of beginning ch-1: 64 sc

Finish off.

September 26: Octopus Holder

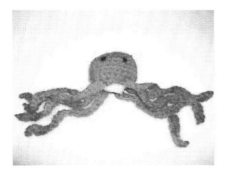

Materials:

Bulky Weight Yarn (40 yards)

Stitch Marker (or scrap of contrasting yarn)

Crochet Hook H (5.00 mm)

Instructions

Round 1: Make an adjustable ring, 8 sc into ring, place marker: 8 sc

Round 2: 2 sc into each sc around: 16 sc

Round 3: (sc into next sc, 2 sc in next sc) 8 times: 24 sc

Rounds 4 – 9: sc in each sc around: 24 sc

Round 10: (sc in next sc, sc2tog) 8 times: 16 sc

Round 11: sc2tog 8 times, sl st in first sc2tog: 8 sc

Finish off.

Tentacles:

Row 1: Ch 13, 2 sc in 2nd ch from hook and each rem ch: 24 sc

Finish off. Sew tentacles to body. If desired, embroider face on octopus.

September 27: Water Bottle Holder

Materials:

Medium Weight Yarn (small amount)

Crochet Hook J (6.00 mm)

Yarn Needle   crochet yarn size 4

crochet water bottle holder

Instructions

Round 1: ch 4, 12 dc in forth ch from hook, sl st in top of beginning ch-4: 12 dc

Round 2: ch 3, 2 dc in each dc around, sl st in top of beginning ch-3: 24 dc

Round 3: (ch 4, skip 2 dc, sc in next dc) around, place marker: 8 sc

Round 4: (ch 4, sc in next ch-4 space) around: 8 sc

Repeat round 4, nine times or unitl water bottle holder is as tall as you desire, then finish off.

Strap

Start by chaining 120 or as long as you want your strap.

Row 1: ch 3, dc in forth ch from hook and in each ch across: 120 dc

Finish off and use a yarn needle to sew each end of the strap to opposite sides of the top of water bottle holder.

September 28: Classic Lanyard

Materials:

Medium Weight Yarn (small amount of main color)

Crochet Hook H (4.00 mm)

Yarn needle

Key ring   crochet yarn size 4

Instructions

Round 1: ch 100 (or a chain that is the circumference of the your desired lanyard. Remember that lanyard will stretch), place the chain though the center of the key ring, sl st in next first ch made: 100 ch

Round 2: ch 2, hdc in each ch around, sl st in top of beginning ch-2: 100 hdc

Round 3: sl st in each hdc around, finish off: 100 sl st

Optional: with a yarn needle, sew a straight line across lanyard 1″ above the key ring. This will prevent the ring from sliding around the lanyard

September 29: Ear Warmer

Materials:

Medium Weight Yarn

Crochet Hook F (3.75mm)

yarn Needle   crochet yarn size 4

crochet earwarmer

Instructions

Round 1: ch 91, sl st in first ch to form loop, place marker

Round 2-5: sc in each sc around

Round 6 – 8: (dc in next sc, chain one, skip one) around

Round 9 – 12: sc in each st around, sl st in next sc, finish off

September 30: Wrist Cuff

Materials:

Medium Weight Boucle Yarn (approximately 50 yards)

Crochet Hook H (5 mm)

Sewing Needle

Sewing Thread

2 Buttons (1″ in diameter)

crochet yarn size 4

Instructions

Row 1: ch 30, dc in fourth ch from hook (beginning ch 3 counts as 1 dc now and throughout) and in each ch across: 27 dc

Row 2-3: ch 3, turn, dc in each dc across: 27 dc

Once you have completed 3 rows, finish off and weave in loose ends.

Finish

October
October 1: Itty Bitty Hat

Materials:

Medium Weight Yarn

Crochet Hook G (4.0 mm)   crochet yarn size 2

Instructions

Round 1: Make adjustable ring, ch 1, 6 sc in ring, sl st in first sc: 6 sc

Round 2: ch 1, 2 sc in each sc around, sl st in first sc: 12 sc

Rounds 3-5: ch 2, hdc in each st around, sl st in first hdc: 12 hdc

Round 6: ch 2, 2 hdc in each hdc around, sl st in first hdc: 24 hdc

Finish off.

October 2: Expanding Pentagon Motif

Materials:

Light Weight Yarn

Crochet Hook B (2.25 mm)

Instructions

Round 1: make an adjustable ring, ch 3 (counts as 1 dc now and throughout), 14 dc in ring, sl st in top of beginning ch-3: 15 dc

Round 2: ch 6, dc in same dc as last sl st, *dc in next 2 dc, (dc, ch 3, dc) in next dc, repeat from * 3 more times, dc in next 2 dc, sl st in third ch of beginning ch-6: 20 dc

Round 3: (sl st, ch 3, dc, ch 3, 2 dc) in first ch-3 space, *dc in next 4 dc, (2 dc, ch 3, 2 dc) in next ch-3 space, repeat from * 3 more times, dc in next 4 dc, sl st in top of beginning ch-3: 40 dc

Round 4: sl st in next dc, (sl st, ch 3, dc, ch 3, 2 dc) in first ch-3 space, *dc in next 8 dc, (2 dc, ch 3, 2 dc) in next ch-3 space, repeat from * 3 more times, dc in next 8 dc, sl st in top of beginning ch-3: 60 dc

Finish off

October 3: Lucky Star Motif

Materials:

Light Weight Yarn

Crochet Hook E (3.50 mm)

Crochet yarn size 2

Instructions

Round 1: make adjustable ring, ch 3, (dc, hdc) 5 times in ring, sl st in first dc: 10 sts

Round 2: ch 7, skip 2 sts, 2 sl st in next dc, (ch 7, skip 1 st, 2 sl st in next st) around until 1 st remains, ch 7, skip 1 st, sl st in first dc of previous round: 35 ch

Round 3: ch 2, hdc in each ch around: 35 sts

Round 4: ch 2, (hdc in next 3 hdc, 3 dc in next hdc, hdc in next 3 hdc) around: 45 sts

Finish off.

October 4: Mini Motif

Materials:

Medium Weight Yarn (12 yards of color A and 5 yards of color B)

Crochet Hook H (5.00 mm)

crochet yarn size 4

Instructions

Round 1: with color A, make an adjustable ring, ch 3 (counts as 1 dc now and throughout), (2 dc, tr, ch 1, tr, [3 dc, tr, ch 1, tr] 3 times) in ring, sl st in beginning ch-3: 24 sts

Round 2: ch 3, dc in next 3 sts, (tr, ch 1, tr) in next ch-1 space, *dc in next 5 sts, (tr, ch 1, tr) in next ch-1 space, repeat from * 2 more times, dc in next st, sl st in top of beginning ch-3: 32 sts

Round 3: ch 1, sc in next 5 sts, 3 sc in next ch-1 space, *sc in next 7 sts, 3 sc in next ch-1 space, repeat from * 2 more times, sc in next 2 sts, sl st in beginning sc: 40 sts

Finish off.

October 5: Concave Motif

Materials:

Medium Weight Yarn

Crochet Hook I (5.50 mm)

Crochet yarn size 4

Instructions

Round 1: Make adjustable ring, ch 3, 12 dc in ring, sl st in top of beginning ch-3: 12 dc

Round 2: ch 1, (sc in next 2 dc, ch 5, skip 1 dc) around, sl st in beginning ch-1: 28 sts

Round 3: ch 1, (sc2tog, 8 hdc in next ch-5 space) around, sl st in beginning ch-1: 36 sts

Round 4: ch 1, (sc in next 4 sts, ch 3, tr2tog, ch 3, sc in next 3 sts) around, sl st in beginning ch-1: 56 sts

Round 5: ch 1, (sc in next 4 sc, 4 sc in next ch-3 space, ch 2, 4 dc in tr, ch 2, 4 sc in next ch-3 space, sc in next 3 sc) around, sl st in beginning ch-1: 92 sts

Finish off.

October 6: Open Star Motif

Materials:

Size 10 crochet thread

Crochet Hook B (2.25 mm)   Yarn size 0

Instructions

Round 1: make adjustable ring, ch 2, 10 hdc in ring, sl st in top of beginning ch-2: 10 hdc

Round 2: ch 1, (sc in next hdc, ch 3, tr in next hdc, ch 3) around, sl st in first sc: 40 st

Round 3: ch 1, (sc in next sc, 3 sc in next ch-space, ch 2, dc in next tr, ch 2, 3 sc in ch-space) around, do not sl st: 60 st

Round 4: ch 1, (sl st in next 4 sc, 2 sc in ch-space, ch 2, dc in next dc, ch 2, 2 sc in ch-space, sl st in next 3 sc) around: 80 st

Finish off.

October 7: Skull Motif

Materials:

Fine Weight Yarn (20 yards)

Contrasting Yarn (Any weight, 1 yard)

Crochet Hook F (3.75mm)

Yarn needle

Instructions

Round 1: Make an adjustable ring, ch 1, make 8 sc in ring, sl st into beginning ch-1: 8 sc

Round 2: ch 1, 2 sc in each sc around, sl st into beginning ch-1: 16 sc

Round 3: ch 1, (2 sc in next sc, sc in next sc) around, sl st into beginning ch-1: 24 sc

Round 4: ch 1, (2 sc in next sc, sc in next sc) around, sl st into beginning ch-1: 36 sc

Work the following in rows, not rounds. Do not finish off, continue with pattern.

Row 1: ch 1, sc in first 8 sc: 8 sc

Rows 2-3: ch 1, turn, sc in each sc across: 8 sc

Finish off.

October 8: Doll Cape

Materials:

Small amount size 10 crochet cotton.

Size 7 steel crochet hook

Tapestry needle

Collar

Instructions

ROW 1: Ch22. Sc in 2nd ch from hook and in each ch across. Ch1, turn.

ROW 2: Sc in first sc. *Sk next sc. Dc, ch3, dc in next sc. Sk next sc. Sc in next sc. Rep from * across. Fasten off and weave ends into work.

Cape

Turn work around so that you will now work on the starting chain on the other side.

ROW 1: Join red on the first st of starting chain. Sc in first ch and in each ch across. Ch4, turn.

ROW 2: Sc in first sc. Ch4. Sk next sc. Sc in next st. *Ch4, sk next st. Sc in next st. Rep from * across. Ch1, turn.

ROW 3: Sc in first sc. *Dc, ch3, dc, ch3, dc in next ch 4 lp. Sc in next sc. Rep from * across.

ROW 4: Sc in first sc. Sc, dc, ch3, dc, sc in each ch3 sp across. Sc in last sc. Ch3, turn.

ROW 5: Dc, ch3, dc in each ch3 sp across. Dc in last sc. Ch1, turn.

ROW 6-18: Repeat rows 4 & 5 until you reach row 18. Fasten off and weave ends into work. You can add a ribbon to the collar if you like. I didn't because it stays on the doll very well without it.

October 9: Rose Earrings

Materials

Size 80 thread

Crochet Hook Size 6

Instructions

SR 4 / 2 P 2

SR 5 / 2 P 2

4SR 6 / 3 P 3

4SR 8 / 4 P 4

5SR 10 / 5 P 5

5SR 14 / 5 P 5

5SR 16 / 6 P 6 leave the ends several inches long so you can tie the end of the last ring to the underside of the rose after gathering.

You should have 25 rings

Thread a needle with the end of shuttle 2 beginning tail. Thread it through P on the lower side of each ring.

Spiral the rings as you thread them on the needle, going through each picot one direction.

Hold the rose tight together and know the thread.

Tie the ends after the 25th ring to one of the other rings

October 10: Blue & White Earrings

Materials

One shuttle

Variegated cotton size 8, color 121

Two 1/2" beads

Two jewelry findings

Instructions

Round 1: 4ds p 4ds close, turn

*Ch: 3ds p (2ds p) 6 times 4ds, do not turn

R: 6ds sp 3ds close

R: 3ds j to last p of previous r 3ds p 2ds lp 2ds p 3ds sp 3ds close

R: 3ds j to last p of previous 6ds close, turn

R: 1ds p (finished length=1/2") 1ds close, turn work

Ch: 4ds p (2ds p) 6 times 3ds

Pull the 1/2" p through the bead and join

Cut and tie through the base of the first ring. Slip an earring hook through the picot on the first ring.

October 11: Ankle Bracelet

Materials

No. 5 needle

Size 10 thread

Beads

Barrel clasp

Instructions

String 9 beads on ball thread.

Thread needle. Leave at least 1½ yards thread before first ds.

R 8 - 8 close.

* Slide 1 bead close to ring. Put needle thread through bead. Snug bead down tight to ring.

SR 8 / 8 close.

Repeat from * until you have all beads and SR. Be sure to end with split ring. RW Cut thread leaving long tails.

Finish.

October 12: Wrist Warmers

Materials:

Medium Weight Yarn

Crochet Hook I (5.50 mm)

Yarn Needle

Crochet yarn size 4

Instructions

Row 1: ch 41, sc in second ch from hook and in each ch across: 40 sc

Row 2: ch 1, turn, sc in back loop only of each sc across: 40 sc

Repeat row 2, 28 times

Use yarn needle to sew sides of wrist warmer together

October 13: Pocket Purse

Materials:

Medium Weight Yarn (approximately 50 yards)

Crochet Hook I (5.50 mm)

3/4″ button (for closure)

Crochet yarn size 4

Instructions

Row 1: ch 15, dc in fourth ch from hook; and in each ch across: 12 dc

Row 2 – 18: ch 3, turn, dc in each dc across: 12 dc

Once you have completed 18 rows, fold the "purse" leaving 5 rows for the flap. Sl st both sides together and finish off.

Finishing

October 14: Eye Glass Caddie

Materials:

Medium Weight Yarn

Crochet Hook G (4.00 mm)

Crochet yarn size 4

Instructions

Row 1: ch 20, hdc in third chain from hook and in each ch across: 18 hdc

Row 2 – 18: ch 2, turn, hdc in each hdc across: 18 hdc

Finish off.

October 15: Envelope

Materials:

Medium Weight Yarn

Crochet Hook I (5.5 mm)

Yarn Needle

Scissors

Crochet yarn size 4

Instructions

Start by chaining 20 or a chain that is the length of the diagonal of the envelope desired

Row 1: ch 1, sc in second ch from hook and in each ch across: 20 sc

Row 2: ch 1, turn, sc in each sc across: 20 sc

Repeat row 2 23 times or repeat until your work is the shape of a square, then finish off.

October 16: Twist Headband

Materials:

Light Weight Yarn

Crochet Hook K (6.50 mm)   crochet yarn size 3

Instructions

Row 1: ch 27, sc in second ch from hook: 1 sc

Row 2: ch 1, turn, 2 sc in first sc: 2 sc

Row 3: ch 1, turn, 2 sc in each sc across: 4 sc

Row 4: ch 3, turn, dc in each dc across: 4 dc

Row 5 – 11: ch 3, turn, dc in each dc across: 4 dc

Row 12: ch 3, turn, dc in first dc, skip 1 dc, bpdc in next dc, bpdc in skipped dc, dc in last dc: 4 dc

Row 13: ch 3, turn, dc in first dc, fpdc in next 2 dc, dc in last dc: 4 dc

Row 14: ch 3, turn, dc in first dc, bpdc in next 2 dc, dc in last dc: 4 dc

Row 15: repeat row 13

Row 16 – 19: repeat rows 12-15

Row 20: repeat row 12

Row 21 – 28: repeat row 5

Row 29: ch 1, turn, sc2tog across: 2 sc

Row 30: ch 1, turn, sc2tog, ch 26: 1 sc

Finish off.

October 17: Rustic Star Ornament

Materials:

Medium Weight Yarn

Crochet Hook G (4.00 mm)

Ribbon for hanging

Crochet yarn size 4

Instructions

Round 1: make an adjustable ring, ch 1, 10 sc in ring, sl st in first sc: 10 sc

Round 2: ch 1, *(sc, dc) in next sc, ch 2, (dc, sc) in next sc, repeat from * around, sl st in first sc: 20 sts

Round 3: ch 1, *sc in next sc, dc in next dc, (2 dc, ch 2, 2 dc) in next ch-2 space, dc in next dc, sc in next sc, repeat from * around, sl st in first sc: 40 sts

Finish off.

Cut about 16" of ribbon, string through one of the star's ch-2 spaces, and tie a bow

October 18: Beaded Circle Pendant

Materials:

Size 5 thread

Crochet Hook B (2.25 mm)

2 seed beads

Stitch marker   crochet yarn size 0

Instructions

Round 1: string beads, make adjustable ring, (8 sc, sc with bead, 8 sc) in ring, place marker: 17 sc

Round 2: (2 sc in next sc, sc in next sc) 4 times, sc in next sc, (sc in next sc, 2 sc in next sc) 4 times: 25 sc

Round 3: (2 sc in next sc, sc in next 2 sc) 4 times, sc with bead in next sc, (sc in next 2 sc, 2 sc in next sc) 4 times: 33 sc

Round 4: sc in each sc around: 33 sc

Finish off.

October 19: Mini Wreath

Materials:

Medium Weight Yarn

Crochet Hook L (8.0 mm)

Crochet yarn size 4

Instructions

Round 1: ch 10, sl st in first ch to form ring, ch 1, working in back loops only (2 sc in next ch, 3 sc in next ch) around, working in front loops only (2 sc in next ch, 3 sc in next ch) around: 50 sc

Round 2: turn, (ch 4, skip 1 sc, sc in next sc) around: 125 sts

Finish off.

October 20: Squircle Earrings

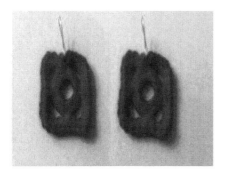

Materials:

Fine Weight Yarn

Crochet Hook B (2.25 mm)

Earwires   Crochet yarn size 2

Instructions

Round 1: make adjustable ring, 12 sc in ring, sl st in first sc: 12 sc

Round 2: (ch 5, skip 3 sc, sl st in next sc) around: 24 sts

Round 3: (sc in next 2 ch, 3 sc in next ch, sc in next 3 sts) around: 32 sc

Finish off. Attach earwires.

October 21: Simple Twist Cuff

Materials:

Medium Weight Yarn

Crochet Hook H (5.00 mm)

Crochet yarn size 4

Instructions

Row 1: ch 9, dc in forth ch from hook and in each ch across: 6 dc

Row 2: ch 3, turn, dc in next 2 dc, skip 1 dc, fpdc in next dc, (with hook in front) fpdc in skipped dc, dc in next 2 dc: 6 dc

Row 3: ch 3, turn, dc in next 2 dc, bpdc in next 2 dc, dc in next 2 dc: 6 dc

Row 4 – 15: repeat rows 2 – 3

Row 16: repeat row 2

Finish off, and seam short ends together.

October 22: Mug Cozy

Materials:

Medium Weight Yarn (approximately 21 yards of color A, 2 yards of colors B and C)

Crochet hook I (5.50 mm)

1 1/2" button or size of your choice

Yarn needle

crochet yarn size 4

Instructions

Row 1: with color A, ch 31, sc in second ch from hook and in each ch across: 30 sc

Row 2: ch 1, turn, sc in each sc across: 30 sc

Row 3: ch 7, turn, (sl st, sc) in first sc, sc in each remaining sc across: 30 sc

Row 4 – 5: ch 1, turn, sc in each sc across: 30 sc

Single crochet evenly around, working two sc in each corner and 8 sc in ch-7 space. Finish off.

October 23: Snowflake Mug Cozy

Materials:

Medium Weight Yarn (approximately 40 yards of color A, 2 yards of color B, and a small amount of color C)

Crochet Hook G (4.00 mm)

Yarn needle

crochet yarn size 4

Instructions

Round 1: with color A, ch 34, sl st to first ch to form ring, being careful not to twist ch, ch 1, sc in each ch around, sl st in first sc: 34 sc

Round 2: skip first sc, (sl st, ch 1, sc) in next sc, sc in each sc around, leaving last sc unworked: 32 sc

Round 3 – 12: ch 1, turn, sc in next 32 sc: 32 sc

Round 13: ch 1, turn, sc in next 32 sc, ch 1, sl st in first sc to join: 32 sc

Round 14: ch 1, turn, sc in each st around, sl st in first sc: 33 sc

Finish off

October 24: Spiral Flower Pattern

Materials:

Medium Weight Yarn (approximately 10 yards)

Crochet Hook G (4.00 mm)   crochet yarn size 4

Instructions

Round 1: make adjustable ring, 6 sc in ring, place marker: 6 sc

Round 2: working in front loops only throughout pattern, 2 sc in each sc around: 12 sc

Round 3: (2 sc in next sc, sc in next sc) around: 18 sc

Round 4: sc in each sc around: 18 sc

Round 5: ch 4, turn, tr in first sc, [tr, ch 4, sl st] in next sc, ([sl st, ch 4, tr] in next sc, tr in next sc, [tr, ch 4, sl st] in next sc) around until center of flower is reached: 18 petals

Finish off

October 25: Beaded Eyewear

Materials:

Super Light Weight Yarn (approximately 10 yards)

Crochet Hook size D (3.25mm)

69 seed beads

Instructions

Row 1: (add all beads to thread and push out of the way) ch 139, sl st in 2nd ch from hook, *ch 1 with bead, skip 1 ch, sl st in next ch, repeat from * until 1 ch remains, ch 1 with bead, sl st in last ch: 70 sl st

Finish off.

October 26: Chair Cushion

Materials:

Medium Weight Yarn (approximately 350 yards)

Crochet Hook G (4.00 mm)

Polyester fiberfill

Yarn needle

Stitch marker crochet yarn size 4

Instructions

Round 1: ch 16, sc in second ch from hook and in each each ch across, turn to work into remaining loops on opposite side of ch, sc in each ch across, place marker: 30 sc

Round 2 – 15: sc in each sc around: 30 sc

Finish off, leaving a long end for sewing. Fill square with fiberfill until it is the firmness that you desire. Then sew the opening of the square shut using a yarn needle.

October 27: Easy Glasses Case

Materials:

Medium Weight Yarn (approximately 50 yards)

Crochet Hook H (5.00 mm)   crochet yarn size 4

Instructions

Start by ch 8 or the width of your desired glasses case

Round 1: ch 2, hdc in third ch from hook and in each ch across, working into remaining loops on opposite side of chain, hdc in each ch across, sl st in top of beginning ch-2: 16 hdc

Round 2: ch 2, turn, hdc in each hdc around, sl st in top of beginning ch-2: 16 hdc

Repeat round 2, 14 times or until the glasses case is as long as you desire. Then finish off.

October 28: Homespun Scarf

Materials:

Bulky Weight Yarn (approximately 185 yards)

Crochet Hook K (6.50 mm)

Instructions

Row 1: ch 18, dc in forth ch from hook and in each ch across: 16 dc

Note: Beginning ch 3 counts as 1 dc

Row 2: ch 3, turn, dc in each dc across: 16 dc

Repeat Row 2 until piece measures your desired length.

October 29: Chunky Chain Scarf

Materials:

Super Bulky Weight Yarn (approximately 50 yards each of colors A and B)

Crochet Hook P (11.50 mm)

Instructions

Row 1: ch 100, finish off.

Hold chains even with each other on one end and knot where the chains begin. Repeat knot for other end.

October 30: Open Tunisian Scarf

Materials:

Fine Weight Yarn (approximately 75 yards)

Tunisian crochet Hook H (5.00 mm) crochet yarn size 2

Instructions

Note: All tdc will be made by inserting hook as if to make a tbs.

Row 1: ch 22, pull up a loop in second ch from hook and in each ch across, work return pass: 21 tss

Row 2: ch 2, (tdc in next 6 sts, yo 4 times, skip 4 sts) until 1 st remains, tdc in last st: 21 sts

Row 3: ch 2, tdc in first st, (yo 4 times, skip 4 sts, tdc in next 6 sts) across: 21 sts

Row 4-69: repeat rows 2-3

Row 70: sl st in each st across: 21 sl st

Finish off.

October 31: Knot Bracelet

Materials:

Cotton yarn in red and white

Knitting doll or 2.5 mm hook

Scissors

Pliers

Chain

 Clasp

7 jump rings

Instructions

Make 2 pieces with red and white yarn.

Round 1: ch 2 and make 6 sc in second ch from hook.

Round 2: sc in each st around

Repeat this process to the desired length. Fasten off and weave in ends.

Fold the tube into half to make a knot; press at the ends and fold your tube

Add jump rings to the four ends and 1 more at each end.

Add your chain and place the last jump ring at the one end of the chain and the clasp at the other end. Done!

November
November 1 Cellphone Cozy

Materials

2 pcs 5-cm extender chain

1 pc 1-cm metal ring

2 pcs 0.75-cm metal ring

1 lobster lock

White sewing thread

Ch 1. (In ch-2 sp, work 1 sc, 1 hdc, 1 dc, 1 tr, 1 dc, 1hdc, and 1 sc. Ch 2, 1 dc in sc of previous row, 1 dc and 1 tr in hdc, 1 tr and 1 dtr in dc, 2 dtr in tr, 1 dtr and 1 tr in dc, 1 tr and 1 dc in hdc, and 1 dc and 1 hdc in sc. Sl st to the nearest sc in stamen.

TURN. Across petal,2 sl st, 10 sc, 2 sl st, sl st to the nearest sc in stamen.) 5x.

Weave in ends.

November 2 Fuzzy Neck Warmer

Materials

1 ball Lion Brand Jiffy

J (6.0 mm) hook

1 ¼ inch button

Yarn needle

Instructions

Ch 13.

Row 1. Sc in 2nd ch from hook and each ch across. Ch 1, turn (12 sc).

Row 2. Working in back loops only, sc in each st across. Ch 1, turn (12 sc).

Repeat row 2 until piece measures 14 ¼ inches.

Next row: Working in back loops only, sc in first 3 sc, ch 6. Skip next 6 sc, sc in last 3 sc. Ch 1, turn (6 sc and 1 ch-6 loop).

Next row: Continuing to work in back loops only, sc in each sc and ch across. Ch 1, turn (12 sc).

Working in back loops only, sc in each sc across for an additional 3 rows.

Finish

November 3 Apple Cozy

Materials

1 Skein of Knit Picks Shine Sport in Cherry

1 Skein of Knit Picks Shine Sport in Fedora

Hook: US F (4mm)

Instructions

With Cherry, ch 2

6 sc in 2nd chain from hook

Inc in each sc – 12 sts

Inc, 1 sc repeat across round - 18 sts

Inc, 2 sc repeat across round – 24 sts

Sc for 2 rounds

Inc, 3 sc repeat across round – 30 sts

Sc for 11 rounds

Finish

November 4 Scarf Pattern

Materials

1.76oz of Worsted Weight #3 Yarn in Main Color

1.76oz of Worsted Weight #3 Yarn in Two Contrast Colors

6.00mm & 5.00mm crochet hooks

Instructions

Scarf - With main color yarn and 6.00mm hook, ch34, change to 5.00mm hook, work 1sc

In 3rd ch from hook, * skip 2ch's, 2sc in next ch, ch2, 2sc in next ch, * repeat from * to * to last 3ch, skip 2ch's, 1sc in last ch. Turn. Fasten off. (7, ch2 spaces)

Join in 1st contrast color

Pattern Row - ch2, 1sc in base of ch2, skip 2sc, * (2sc, ch2, 2sc) in next ch2 space, skip 4sc, * repeat from * to * to last 3sc and ch2, skip 3sc, 1sc in top of ch2. Turn. Repeat last row nine more times. Turn. Fasten off. (7 groups)

Join in main color, repeat last row three more times. Fasten off.

Repeat Pattern Row in color sequence as follows:-

10 rows 2nd contrast color. Fasten off

3 rows main color. Fasten off

10 rows 1st contrast color. Fasten off

3 rows main color # Fasten off

Repeat color sequence from # to # 4 more times until 144 rows have been worked in all or

Work measures 47 Inches from beginning. DNT or fasten off at the end of the last row

November 5 Abstract Autumn Scarf

Materials

1 ball of 4 ply yarn

Size G crochet hook

Instructions

Chain 6, join, chain 6 (in loop made by first ch 6) repeat 4 times for a total of 5 ch6 and 5 sc.

Foundation single crochet (fsc) * scroll down for videos 2 and 4 where you can see how to do fsc* repeat Beginning motif Sl into a close ch 6 loop

fsc, repeat motif, sl into a nearby ch 6

Continue until you have 60 motifs or have the length you desire

November 6 Scarflet

Materials

Red Heart worsted weight yarn Cherry Red (scraps)

Crochet hook size H

Scissors

Instructions

Ch 64.

Row 1- 1 dc in fourth ch from hook and in each ch across. Ch 3, turn. (62 dc)

Row 2- 1 dc in each dc across. Ch 3, turn. (62 dc)

Row 3- 1 dc in each dc across. Ch 3, turn. (62 dc)

Row 4- 1 dc in each dc across. Fasten of Cherry Red, weave in tail. (62 dc)

Row 5- Join Ranch Red and work 1 dc in each dc across. Ch 3, turn. (62 dc)

Row 6- 1 dc in each dc across. Ch 3, turn. (62 dc)

Row 7- 1 dc in each dc across. (62 dc) Fasten off Ranch Red. Weave in tails.

Row 8- Join Claret to foundation loops of first Cherry Red row. Work 1 sc in each dc across. (62 sc) Ch 1, turn.

Row 9- Work 17 sc across narrow side of scarflet.

Row 10- Working on long side of scarflet (Ranch Red side), make 62 sc.

Row 11- Work 17 sc across opposite narrow side of scarflet. Sl st to join to beginning sc

November 7 Ridged Scarf

Materials:

Worsted Weight Yarn. Red Heart Super Saver Yellow.

Size J crochet hook

Instructions

Chain 22

ROW 1 - In third chain stitch from your hook, single crochet (sc). SC in the rest of the chains to the end. Turn.

ROW 2 - In each SC across, SC in the front loops only. Turn.

Repeat ROW 2 until the scarf is about 55-60 inches long.

Bind off and weave in any loose yarn ends

November 8 Lemonade Scarf Pattern

Materials:

Knitting Boucle Yarn - approximately 3 ounces.

Each skein had 1.7 ounces and the

Hook Size NR1

Instructions

Ch17, dc in 4th ch from hook. Dc in each remaining ch. (15dc)

R2: Ch3, turn. Dc in next 2 dc. (Ch3, sk 3dc, dc in next 3dc) twice.

R3: Ch3, turn. Dc in next 2dc. 3dc in ch-3 sp. Ch3, sk 3dc. 3dc in ch-3 sp. Dc in last 3dc.

R4: Ch3, turn. Dc in next 2dc. Ch3, sk 3dc. 3dc in ch-3 sp. Ch3, sk 3dc. Dc in last 3dc.

Rs 5-64: Alternate repeating Rows 3 and 4. (You can make the scarf any length you want).

Last Row: Dc in ea dc and place 3dc in ea ch-3 sp.

Fasten Off.

November 9 Infinity Scarf

Materials

Medium Weight Yarn

J/10-6.00 MM Crochet Hook

Yarn Needle

Instructions

Row 1: CH 27. Turn. Skip 3 CH. {DC, CH 1, DC}-into next CH. **Skip 2 CH. {DC, CH 1, DC}-into next CH. Repeat from ** six more times. Skip 1 CH. DC into last CH.

Row 2: CH 3. Turn. 3-DC-CL into CH space of V stitch. **CH 2. 3-DC-CL into CH space of next V stitch. Repeat from ** six more times. CH 1. DC into 2nd CH of CH 3.

Row 3: CH 3. Turn. **{DC, CH 1, DC}- into CH just to the right of the cluster stitch. (See photo below for guidance) Repeat from ** 7 more times. CH 1. DC into 2nd CH of CH 3.

Repeat rows 2 and 3 until desired length. I made mine 4 feet long and had yarn to spare.

November 10 Lightning Scarf

Materials:

5.0 mm hook (H)

Approx. 320 yards Worsted Yarn

Instructions

Ch 2; in 2nd chain from hook, 2 hdc

Ch 2, turn, 1 hdc in each st (2 sts)

Ch 2, turn, 2 hdc in each st (written 2hdcinc) (4 sts)

Ch 2, turn, 1 hdc across (4 sts)

Ch 2, turn, 1 hdc, 2hdcinc twice, 1 hdc (6 sts)

Ch 2, turn, hdc across for 3 rows

Ch 2, turn, 1 hdc, 2hdcinc, 1 hdc twice, 2hdcinc, 1 hdc (8 sts)

Ch 2, turn, hdc across for 6 rows

Ch 2, turn, 1 hdc, 2hdcinc, 1 hdc in next 4 sts, 2hdcinc, 1 hdc (10sts)

Ch 2, turn, hdc across for 6 rows

November 11 Lime Green Cowl

Materials

2 skeins 6 weight super chunky yarn

Size N crochet hook

Instructions

Ch 32

You will be working in a continuous round.

Round 1: Hdc in 3rd ch from hook and in each ch to the end.

When you finish working into the beginning ch do not attach with sl st.

Round 2: Hdc in first hdc worked...this will form the circle. You are now basically working hdc in a continuous spiral.

Do at least 15 rounds

Finish off and weave ends.

November 12 Tab Cowl

Materials:

Worsted Weight Yarn of Choice: Lion Brand Heartland - 2 Skeins in Color-way of choice

1 skein = {5 oz / 251 yards - Worsted Weight (4)}

Hook size: H - (5.00 mm)

Tapestry Needle

Instructions

Round 1: ch 132, join with a sl st to 1st ch but take care not to twist the chs (132)

Round 2: ch 1, sc in same st as join, ch 3, 3dc cl in next ch, ch1, sk 2 chs, *(sc in next ch, ch 3, 3dc cl in next ch, ch1 sk 2 chs) rep from * around, join with a sl st to 1st sc, ch 2, turn (33 - 3dc cl)

Round 3: *(sc, ch 3, 3dc cl) in next ch 3 sp, ch 1, rep from * around, join with a sl st to 1st sc, ch 2, turn

(33 - 3dc cl)

Round 4-14: Rep Round 3, (End of Round 14 do not ch 2, turn at end)

Fasten off and Weave in ends

November 13 Beautiful Angel Barbie Head

Materials

Size G Crochet Hook

3-ply sport weight yarn or Caron yarn

Instructions

Chain 4, join.

Round 1: 12 SC in the loop, do not join. This head will be worked in a continual round.

Round 2: 1 SC on ea SC around. (12 single crochet total)

Round 3: *Work 1 SC in ea of the next 2, Work 2 SC in the same stitch. Complete 4 times total from *. (16 SC total)

Round 4-5: 1 SC in ea SC around (16 single crochet total)

Round 6: Work 8 SC DEC

Stuff the head with fiberfill. Whip stitch around the 8 stitches and pull the opening closed. Sew the head to the top of the dress

November 14 Baby Powder Cover

Materials

Size I Needle

Red heart super saver yarn

Ribbon for the draw string.

A foot yarn, needle and stitch marker.

Instructions

Ch. 2

Rnd1:12 Hdc in 2nd ch from hook, join with sl st in top of 2nd chain (you should have 12 hdc)

Rnd2: ch2, Hdc in ssame st. Then do 2 Hdc in each st around, join (24 stitches)

Rnd 3-21 +/-: Ch2, hdc in each st around. Dont join just keep working in the round using a stitch marker to count the rows.

Finishing: Use a yarn needle to thred the ribbon through the top row of stitches weaving in and out every 2 stitches. Tie off in a bow.

November 15 Coaster Crochet Pattern

Materials:

4 Ply Cotton Yarn (Peaches and Cream-white)

4 Ply Worsted Weight Yarn (Simply Soft -Brocade Print 9810)

Hook Size H

Instructions

Round1: Ch 16, sc in 2nd ch from hook.

(Ch1, sk next ch, sc in next ch) across. Ch1, turn.

Round2: Sc in ea sc and ch-sp across. Ch1, turn.

Round3: Sc in 1st st. Ch1, sk next st, sc in ea st across to last 2 sts.

Sk next st. Sc in last st.

Round4-15: Alternate repeating R2 and R3, ending with R2.

Round16: Ch1, turn. Sc in 1st st. (Ch1, sk next st. Sc in next st) across.

BORDER: Sc evenly in every st and ch-sp around placing 3sc in every corner.

Fasten off.

November 16 Penny Coaster

Materials

Brown yarn

H hook.

Instructions

Round 1: Ch 4 join with ss to first ch

Round 2: Ch 3 and do 11 dc in loop join with ss to first dc; ch 3

Round 3-4: 2 dc in each st join with ss to ch 3

Round 5: 1 dc in each st; join with ss; ch 1

Round 6: 1 sc in each st join with ss and fasten off.

November 17 29 Stitch Dishcloth

Materials

100% Cotton yarn

Size "H" hook

Instructions

Ch 30

sc in 2nd ch from hook and in each ch across, ch 2, turn. (29 stitches)

sc in 1st sc, *sk 1 sc, (dc and sc) in next sc, repeat from * across, ch 2, turn.

sc in 1st sc, *sk next dc, (dc and sc) in next sc, repeat from * across, ch 2, turn.

Repeat row 3 until desired length. (Mine measures 8 1/2 inches.)

Border

sc evenly around cloth, (3 sc) in each corner, sl st to beg sc, ch 1, do not turn work.

rev sc evenly around cloth, sl st to beg rev sc, fasten off.

Weave in ends.

November 18 Magic dishcloth pattern

Materials

"H" (5 mm) Crochet Hook

2 ozs of Cotton yarn

1/4 oz contrasting Cotton yarn for trim

Instructions

Row 1: Ch 32, Sc in 2nd ch from hook and in ea st. (31)

Row 2: (DC Row) Ch 2, turn. DC in 1st st, *Ch 1, Sk next st, DC in next st*

Repeat between * to end. Work another DC in last st.

Row 3: (SC Row)

Ch 1, turn. Sk 1st DC, *Sc in next DC, Sc in Ch 1 sp, Sc in next DC*

Repeat between * to last st of row. Sk last DC and Sc into the top of Ch 2.

Repeat Row 2 and 3 until have 10 rows of boxes. End with row 3. FO.

November 19 Slouchy Hat

Materials

80 grams (about 150 yards)

I hook

Instructions

ch1

Round 1: 8sc in the ch1, join but don't turn.

Round 2: ch 5, sc in each stitch around. Join and don't turn.

Round 3: Ch1 and 5sc in each loop all the way around. Join and don't turn.

Round 4: ch5 and sc in the third sc of each loop. Work until you get to the last loop. Ch2 and dc in the starting st. Turn.

Round 5: (ch5, sc in the loop space) around until last loop then ch 2, dc, turn

Rounds 6-10: Repeat round 5.

Round 11: (ch5, sc) around in both loop and sc of previous row.

Rounds 12-23: Repeat round 5.

Round 24: (ch1, sc in lp) around. Join and turn.

Round 25-26: Work all sts in sc, join and turn.

Round 27: Ch 2. Sc, dc (moss st) around ending on sc. Join and turn.

Round 28-29: repeat rounds 25-26. Break off, weave in ends.

November 20 Curtain Tie Back

Materials: Worsted weight yarn, any two colors or two strands of one color, as you use two strands held together throughout.

Size K hook.

Instructions

Row 1: Chain 54. Double crochet in fourth chain from hook - chain 3 counts as first DC now and throughout. DC in each chain to the end. 50 DC. Chain 3, turn.

Row 2: DC in second stitch, and each stitch to end. Chain 1. Holding ends together, SC in end of each row, 4 sc made. Fasten off. This crochets the two ends together to form the loop.

November 21 Badge Holder

Materials:

Caron Jewel Box yarn, G hook

Instructions

Row 1: With yarn and G hook ch-3, hdc 2nd ch from hook, hdc next ch, ch-1, turn. (2 sts)

Row 2: Hdc ea st across, ch-1, turn.

Rep row 2 until piece will fit easily over your head, do not fasten off.

Place ends of piece tog and working through both thickness, hdc ea st across, ch-1, turn. (2 sts)

Rep row 2, twice.

Next row: hdc dec 2 sts tog as 1, ch-1, turn.

Next row: hdc only st, fasten off.

November 22 Pen Holder

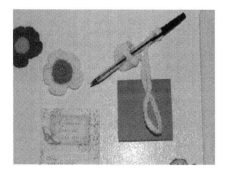

Materials

Small amount of medium or light weight yarn

Hook appropriate for your yarn (I used Red Heart medium weight yarn and a size 5 (H/8) hook)

Magnet strong enough to hold a pen

Hot glue

Instructions:

Ch 10

Row 1: Pull up a loop in the second ch from the hook and in the next four chs. YO, pull through all 6 loops on hook, ch 1 to complete the first star. Pull up a loop in the center of the first star, in the last ch used in the first star, and in the next three chs. YO, pull through all 6 loops on hook. Ch 1 to complete the second star. In final ch, hdc. Ch 2, turn.

Row 2: Three hdc in the center of each star. In the final space, hdc. (7 hdc) Ch 1, turn sideways.

2 Row 1: Along the side of the piece, sc 4 times. Ch 1, turn.

2 Row 2: Sc in each sc across (4 sc)

2 Row 3: Repeat 2 Row 2.

2 Row 4: Fold over. (Looks like a pocket) Slip stitch through both ends across 4 st, ch 1.

Pen chain: Sl st through the corner of both sides, ch 50 (or as many as it takes to get to the length you want for the cord on the pen, plus 5.) Sl st in the fifth ch from the hook, finish off. Weave in ends.

November 23 Fancy Cowl

Material

Bulky weight size 5 yarn

Size M or N crochet hook

Yarn needle

Instructions

Do not crochet too tightly

Work in rounds

The first Ch 2 or Ch 3 of each round counts as the first stitch.

Ch 78 loosely

Join ch with sl st

Rnd 1: Ch 2, hdc in next ch and each ch around. Join with sl st to first st of the rnd.

Rnd 2: Ch 3, Dc in next st and each st around. Join with sl st to first st of the rnd.

Rnds 3 - 8: Repeat rnd 2.

Rnd 9: Ch 2, hdc in each stitch around.

Finish off and weave ends.

November 24 Easy Neck Warmer

Materials:

Super Bulky Weight Yarn

Crochet Hook N (10.00 mm)

Instructions

Round 1: ch 40 (or a chain that can fit over your head), sl st in first ch made forming a loop, be sure not to twist chain: 40 ch

Round 2: ch 3, dc in each ch around, sl st in top of beginning ch-3: 40 dc

Round 3: ch 3, dc in each dc around, sl st in top of beginning ch-3: 40 dc

Repeat round 3, five times or until the neck warmer is as tall as you desire.

November 25 Offset Back scrubber

Materials:

Sugar and Cream Cotton

Size K hook

Blunt needle

Instructions

Chain 36 stitches

Row 1: 1 SC in second chain from hook and in each across (35 stitches)

Row 2 & 4: Chain 1 (counts as first SC), turn. 1 SC in the first ST *1 TR in the next ST. SC in next ST.* Repeat across. (35 stitches)

Row 3, 5, 7 & 9: Chain 1, turn. SC in each ST across.

Row 6 & 8: Chain 1, turn. 1 SC in each of the first 2 stitches, *1 TR in the next ST. SC in next ST.* Repeat across. (35 stitches)

SC around border, tie off.

November 26 Open Ridge Washcloth

Materials

Hook: G/4.0 mm

Yarn; cotton or linen

Instructions:

Chain 36 loosely.

Row 1: Sc in 2nd chain from hook, and 1 sc in ea ch to end. Turn.

Row 2: Ch 1, skip first sc, * skip next sc, hdc in next st, 1 hdc in space between last 2 st., * repeat from *to *, ending with 1 hdc in last sc. Turn.

Row 3: Ch 1, 1 sc in back loop of ea st, end with sc in the ch 1. Turn.

Repeat rows 2 and 3 until the cloth's length is equal to its width, or to your desired size. End with row 3. Turn.

Row 1: Ch 1, 1 sc in ea st across, 3 sc in the last stitch for a corner, sc evenly along each of the sides, continuing to place 3 sc in ea corner st. Sl st to first sc. Turn.

Row 2: Ch 1, 1 sc in first st of corner, place 3 sc in middle st of the corner, 1 sc in third st of corner, and continue 1sc in each st, and 3 sc in the middle st of each corner. Sl st to first sc. Fasten off.

November 27 Bath Milt Single Crochet

Materials

US – I, 5.50mm hook

70 yds total (1.4 oz) Worsted Weight cotton

Yarn/tapestry needle

Instructions

Row 1: Ch 18, sc in the 2nd ch from the hook and each remaining ch across. Turn. (17 sts)

Row 2: Ch1, sc in the 1st st. *Psc in the next st, sc in the next st. Repeat from * to end. Turn. (17 sts)

Row 3: Ch 1, sc in each st to end. Turn. (17 sts)

Row 4: Ch 1, sc in the first 2 sts. *Psc in the next st, sc in the next st. Repeat from * until 1 st remains. Sc in the last st. Turn. (17 sts)

Row 5: Repeat Row 3.

Rows 6 – 21: Repeat Rows 2 – 5 four more times. Break yarn and use the needle to weave in ends.

November 28 Comfortable bath loofah

Materials:

35 g Bernat Cool Crochet

Size I9 (5.5mm) crochet hook

Yarn needle

Instructions:

ch 4, form a ring by joining with a sl st in first st

ch 40

sl st into center of ring (this forms the loop for hanging the loofah)

R1: ch2, dc 4o into center of ring, join with sl st (4o st)

R2: ch2, dc 3 in each st around, join with sl st (120 st)

R3: ch2, dc 3 in each st around, join with sl st (360 st)

R4: ch2, dc 3 in each st around, join with sl st (1080 st)

Bind off. Weave in ends.

November 29 Bathroom Rug

Materials

Mercerized Cotton thread 15 balls each of White and Black.

Plastic Rug Hook - Size G

Instructions

Make a chain 36" long.

Row 1: Sc in 2nd ch from hook and in each ch across until row measures 24 inches, having an even number of sc. Ch 1, turn.

Row 2: Sc in first sc. * sc in base of next sc (long sc made) sc in next sc. Repeat from * across, ending with long sc. Ch 1, turn.

Repeat 2nd row until piece measures 36 inches. Break off.

November 30 Easy Bath Puff

Materials

2 – 2 0z. Yarn

Size "J" hook

Instructions

Ch 40, sl st in first ch

Rnd 1: ch 3, work as many dc in 1st ch as possibly (try for at least 20), join w/ sl st to 3rd beg ch

Rnd 2-3: ch 3, 5 dc in same st, 6 dc in ea dc around, join w/ sl st to 3rd beg ch

Finish off and weave in ends.

December

December 1: Mini Santa Hat

Materials:

Size 10 thread; 5 yards for each color

Crochet Hook 2.25 mm crochet yarn size 0

Instructions:

Row1: with white, ch 16, sl st in first ch and create a loop, ch 3, 3-dc bobble in each ch around: 16 bobbles

Row 2-3: with red, ch 2, hdc in each st around: 16 hdc

Row4: ch 2, (hdc in next 2 hdc, hdc2tog) around: 12 hdc

Row5: ch 2, hdc in each hdc around: 12 hdc

Row6: ch 2, (hdc2tog, hdc in next hdc) around: 8 hdc

Row7: ch 2, hdc in each hdc around: 8 hdc

Row8: ch 2, hdc2tog around: 4 hdc

Row9: ch 2, hdc in each hdc around: 4 hdc

Insert the hook through top of hat, make a 5-dc bobble with white thread.

Finish.

December 2: Barbie Doll Santa Claus Hat

Materials:

Medium Weight Yarn (red & white)

Crochet Hook I (5.50 mm)

Yarn needle

Crochet yarn size 4

Instructions:

Row1: with red, ch 2, 4 sc in second ch from hook, place marker: 4 sc

Row2: sc in each sc around: 4 sc

Row3: 2 sc in each sc around: 8 sc

Row4: sc in each sc around: 8 sc

Row5: (2 sc in next sc, sc in next sc) around: 12 sc

Row6: sc in each sc around: 12 sc

Row7: (2 sc in next sc, sc in next 2 sc) around: 16 sc

Row8 – 9: sc in each sc around: 16 sc

Row10: sc in each sc around, changing to white in last sc made: 16 sc

Row11: sc in each sc around, finish off: 16 sc

December 3: Bobble Bowl

Materials:

80-Yard Bulky Weight Yarn

Crochet Hook K (6.50 mm)

Row 1-3 measure 3½″ in diameter.

Instructions:

Row1: Make an adjustable ring, ch 1, 8 sc into ring, sl st in top of beginning ch: 8 sc

Row2: Ch 2, 2 hdc in each dc around, sl st in top of beginning ch-2: 16 hdc

Row3: Ch 2, 2 hdc in each hdc around, sl st in top of beginning ch-2: 32 hdc

Row4: Ch 2, (2 hdc in next hdc, hdc in next hdc) around, sl st in top of beginning ch-2: 48 hdc

Rounds 5-6: Ch 3, dc in each hdc around, sl st in top of beginning ch-3: 48 dc

Row7: Ch 3, (bo in next dc, dc in next 3 dc) around, sl st in top of beginning ch-3: 48 dc

Row8: Ch 3, dc in next 2 dc, (bo in next dc, dc in next 3 dc), until one stitch remains, dc in last dc, sl st in top of beginning ch-3: 48 dc

Row9: Ch 3, dc in each dc around, sl st in top of beginning ch-3: 48 dc

Finish.

December 4: Winter Chill Christmas Ornament

Materials:

Light Weight Yarn (approximately 16 yards)

Crochet Hook G (4.00 mm)

8½" ball ornament

Instructions:

Row 1: sc in second ch from hook and in each ch across: 8 sc

Row 2 – 9: ch 1, turn, sc in each sc across: 8 sc

Finish.

Row 1: ch 18, sl st in first ch to form a ring, ch 1, sc in first ch, *ch 5, skip 2 ch, (sc, ch 3, sc) in next ch, repeat from * 4 more times, ch 5, skip 2 ch, sc in first ch, ch 3, sl st in first sc: 6 ch-5 spaces

Row 2: sl st in next 2 ch, sc in next ch, *ch 7, (sc, ch 3, sc) in third ch of next ch-5 space, repeat from * 4 more times, ch 7, sc in same ch as first sc, ch 3, sl st in first sc: 6 ch-7 spaces

Row 3: sl st in next 3 ch, sc in next ch, *ch 5, (sc, ch 3, sc) in forth ch of next ch-7 space, repeat form * 4 more times, ch 5, sc in same ch as first sc, ch 3, sl st in first sc: 6 ch-5 spaces

Row 4: sl st in next 2 ch, sc in next ch, *ch 4, (sc, ch 3, sc) in third ch of next ch-5 space, repeat from * 4 more times, ch 4, sc in same ch as first sc, ch 3, sl st in first sc: 6 ch-4 spaces

Row 5: sl st in next ch, sc in next ch, *ch 3, sc in next ch-4 space, repeat from * 4 more times, ch 3, sl st in first sc: 6 ch-3 spaces

Slip around the ornament and continue.

Row 6: sl st in next ch, sc in next ch, *ch 1, sc in next ch-3 space, repeat from * 4 more times, ch 3, sl st in first sc: 6 ch-1 spaces

Finish.

December 5: Christmas Pickle

Materials:

15-Yard Fine Weight Yarn

Crochet Hook E (3.5 mm)

Crochet yarn size 4

Instructions

Row1: Make adjustable ring, 6 sc in ring: 6 sc

Row2: (2 sc in next sc, sc in next sc) around: 9 sc

Rounds 3 – 4: sc in each sc around: 9 sc

Row5 – 7: (3-sc front pc in next sc, sc in next 2 sc) around: 9 sts

Row8: (sc in next 2 sc, 3-sc front pc in next sc) around: 9 sts

Rounds 9 – 10: sc in each sc around: 9 sc

Row 11: (sc2tog, sc in next sc) around: 6 sc

Stuff (optional) then draw closed and finish off

December 6: Christmas Tree Ornament Stuffed

Materials:

30-Yards per color, Medium Weight Yarn

Crochet Hook G (4.25 mm)

Polyester Fiberfill

Crochet yarn size 4

Instruction

Row1: : Make an adjustable ring, ch 3, 10 dc in ring, sl st in top of beg ch-3: 10 dc

Row2: ch 3, 2 dc in each dc around, sl st in top of beg ch-3: 20 dc

Row3: ch 3, working in back loops only now and through-out, dc in each dc around, sl st in top of beg ch-3: 20 dc

Row4: ch 3, (dc in next 3 dc, dc2tog) around, sl st in top of beg ch-3: 16 dc

Row5: ch 3, (dc2tog, dc in next 2 dc) around, sl st in top of beg ch-3: 12 dc

Row6: ch 3, (dc in next 2 dc, dc2tog) around, sl st in top of beg ch-3: 9 dc

Fill with fiberfill before drawing end through the tops of the stitches and finishing off.

Tiers

Ch 3, working in front loops only, 2 dc in each dc aRowin rows 2-5. Finish off after each tier.

You can add more tiers

December 7: Christmas Wreath Applique

Materials:

Red Fingering Yarn (approximately 2 yards)

Green Fingering Yarn (approximately 2 1/2 yards)

Crochet Hook 7 (1.50 mm)

Red Thread

Needle

Scissors

Instructions

Wreath (1)

Row1: with green, ch 12, sl st in first chain made to form a ring, ch 3, 30 dc into ring, sl st in top of beginning ch-3: 30 dc

Finish off.

Bow (2)

Row 1: with red, ch 18, sc in second ch from hook each in each ch across: 17 sc

Finish.

December 8: 3 Holly Berries

Materials:

Red Fingering Yarn (approximately 3 yards)

Green Fingering Yarn (approximately 4 yards)

Crochet Hook 7 (1.50 mm)

Thread

Needle

Scissors

Instructions

Row1: with red, ch 4, sl st in first chain made to form a ring, ch 1, 10 sc in ring, sl st in top of beginning ch-1: 10 sc

Row2: ch 1, 2 sc in each sc around, sl st in top of beginning ch-1: 20 sc

Finish.

December 9: 3 Holly Leaves

Materials:

Red Fingering Yarn (approximately 3 yards)

Green Fingering Yarn (approximately 4 yards)

Crochet Hook 7 (1.50 mm)

Thread

Needle

Scissors

Instructions

Row 1: with green, ch 3, sc in second ch from hook, 2 sc in next ch, ch 1, turn: 3 sc

Row 2-5: sc in each sc across until 1 sc remains, 2 sc in last sc, ch 1, turn

Row 6-7: skip first sc, sc in next sc and in each sc across, ch 1, turn

Row 8-9: sc in each sc across until 1 sc remains, 2 sc in last sc, ch 1, turn

Finish.

December 10: Christmas Ball Ornaments

Materials:

Medium Weight Yarn (small amount)

Crochet Hook F (3.75 mm)

Polyester Fiberfill

Crochet yarn size 4

Gauge: Rounds 1 – 5 in pattern measures 2″ in diameter.

Crochet Pattern: Ornament

Instructions

Row1: ch 2, 6 sc in second ch from hook, place marker: 6 sc

Row2: 2 sc in each sc around: 12 sc

Row3: (2 sc in next sc, sc in next sc) around: 18 sc

Row4: (2 sc in next sc, sc in next 2 sc) around: 24 sc

Row5: (2 sc in next sc, sc in next 3 sc) around: 30 sc

Row6 – 10: sc in each sc around: 30 sc

Row11: (decrease, sc in next 3 sc) around: 24 sc

Row12: (decrease, sc in next 2 sc) around: 18 sc

Row13: (decrease, sc in next sc) around: 12 sc

Fill it with fiberfill.

Row14: decrease around: 6 sc

Row15: ch 25, skip 2 sc, sl st in next sc: finish off.

December 11: Daisy Coaster

Materials:

Worsted Weight Yarn (approximately 6 yards of color A and 12 yards of color B)

Crochet Hook I (5.50 mm)   crochet yarn size 4

Instructions

Row1: with color A, make adjustable double ring (but loop over finger loosely 4 more times), ch 3 (counts as 1 dc), 11 dc in ring, sl st in top of beginning ch-3: 12 dc

Row2: ch 2 (counts as 1 hdc), hdc in same st, 2 hdc in each dc around, join color B with sl st in top of beginning ch-2: 24 hdc

Row3: ch 1, *(dc, tr) in next st, dtr in next st, (tr, dc) in next st, sl st in next st, repeat from * around, make the last sl st in beginning ch-1: 36 sts

Row4: ch 1, *sc in next st, 2 sc in each of next 3 sts, sc in next st, sl st in next st, repeat from * around, make the last sl st in beginning ch-1: 54 sts

Finish.

December 12: Sunny Day Coaster

Materials:

Medium Weight Yarn (approximately 10 yards)

Crochet Hook H (5.0 mm)   crochet yarn size 4

Instruction

Row1: make adjustable ring, ch 3, 10 dc in ring, sl st in top of beg ch-3: 10 dc

Row2: ch 3, 2 dc in each dc around, sl st in top of beg ch-3: 20 sc

Row3: ch 3, (2 dc in next dc, dc in next dc) around, sl st in first dc: 30 sc

Row4: ch 4, tr in second dc, picot in tr, (ch 4, sl st in next 2 dc, ch 4, tr in next dc, picot in tr) 9 times, ch 4, sl st in last dc: 114 sts

Finish.

December 13: Ruffled Coaster

Materials:

Bulky Weight Yarn (approximately 35 yards)

Crochet Hook I (5.5 mm)

Crochet Hook J (6.0 mm)

Crochet yarn size 4

Instruction

Row1: with size I hook, make an adjustable ring, ch 1, 8 sc in ring, sl st in beg ch-1 to join: 8 sc

Row2: ch 3, 2 dc in each sc around, sl st in top of beg ch: 16 dc

Row3: ch 3, (2 dc in each of next 3 dc, dc in next dc) around, sl st in top of beg ch: 28 dc

Row4: With size J hook, ch 3, (2 dc in next dc, ch 1), sl st in top of beg ch: 84 sts

Finish.

December 14: Wheel Coaster

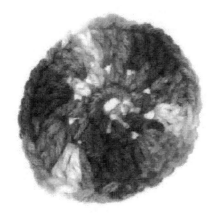

Materials:

Medium Weight Yarn (approximately 25 yards)

Crochet Hook I (5.50 mm)

Instruction:

Row1: ch 5, sl st in first ch made to form a ring, 10 sc in ring: 10 sc

Row2: ch 3 (beginning ch 3 counts as 1 dc now and throughout), dc in each sc around, sl st in first dc joining to beginning of round: 11 dc

Row3: ch 3, 2 dc in space between ch-3 and first dc on Row2, (ch 1, 3 dc) in space between each dc around, sl st in first dc joining to beginning of round: 33 dc

Finish

December 15: Openwork Tie

Material

Crochet cotton size 10: 150 yards.

Steel crochet hook size 7

Two safety pins

Instructions

Pattern note: Ch 2 to start each hdc

Row 1: Ch 22, hdc in 3rd ch from hook and in rem ch across, turn.

Row 2: Ch 1, sc in first hdc {ch 3, sk 1 hdc, sc in next hdc] across, turn. (10 loops)

Row 3: Ch 1, make sc, ch 3 and sc in each lp across, turn. Rep Row 3 until piece measures 25 inches long.

Row 4: Ch 1, sc in each ch-3 lp across, turn. (10 sc)

Mark each end of Row 4 with a safety pin.

Row 5: Ch 2, hdc in each sc across, turn. Rep Row 5 until piece from safety pins measures 27 inches, fasten.

Weave in loose end.

December 16: Berny Stitch Tie

Materials:

2 oz. sport yarn

C hook

Instruction

Ch 11

Base Row:

1 sc in 2nd ch from hook, 1 sc in each ch to end. 10 sts. Turn.

1st Row:

Ch1, 1 sl st in next st, *yo, insert hook in next st, yo and draw through a loop, yo and draw through first loop on hook (3 loops on hook), yo, insert hook in same st, yo and draw through first 4 loops on hook (2 loops on hook), yo and draw through 2 loops on hook - called Berry 1 or B1 -, sl st in next st, rep from * to last 2 sts, B1 in next st, 1 sc in turning ch. Turn.

2nd Row:

Ch1, 1 sl st in each berry st and 1 sc in each sl st to end, ending with 1 sc in turning ch. Turn.

3rd Row:

Ch 1, *B1 in next st, sl st in next st, rep from * to last st, 1 sc in turning ch. Turn.

4th Row:

Ch 1, 1 sc in each sl st and 1 sl st in each berry st to end, ending with 1 sc in turning ch. Turn.

1st to 4th rows from pattern.

Repeat pattern until work measures 52:, ending with a 2nd row.

Fasten.

December 17: Crochet Men's Bowtie

Materials

Steel crochet hook size 4

Crochet cotton 200 yards

Instruction

Strap: Measure around neck and ch until reaches length. turn.

Row 1: sc in 2nd ch from hook and across. turn

Row 2: ch1, sc in first sc and across. turn

Repeat 4 more times. Fasten off. Sew in ends.

Bow: ch 28 turn.

Row 1: sc in 2nd ch from hook and across

Row 2: ch1, sc in first sc. and across. Repeat 11 more times. Fasten off. Sew in ends

Center: Ch 10 turn.

Row 1: ch1, sc in first sc, and across. Repeat 3 more times. Fasten off. Sew in ends.

December 18: Shell Stitch Tie

Materials

Crochet cotton size 10: 200 yds. desired color

Steel crochet hook size 7

Two safety pins

Instructions

Row 1: Ch 20, sc in 2nd ch from hook {sk 2 ch, 5 dc in next ch, sk 2 ch] 3 times, turn.

Row 2: Ch 3, 2 dc in first sc, sk 2 st, sc in next dc {sk 2 st, 5 dc in next sc, sk 2 st, sc in next dc] 2 times, sk 2 st, 3 dc in next sc, turn.

Row 3: Ch 1, sc in first dc {sk 2 st, 5 dc in next sc, sk 2 st, sc in next dc] 3 times, turn.

Rep Rows 2-3 for pattern until piece measures 25 inches from beginning, ending with Row 3.

Row 4: Ch 3, make fill-in shell stitch over next 3 sts [fill-in shell over next 6 sts] 2 times, fill-in shell over last 3 sts, turn.

Row 5: Ch 3, make 9 dc evenly across Row, turn. (10) Mark each side at base of Row 5 with safety pins.

Row 6: Ch 3, dc in each dc across, turn. Rep Row 6 until piece from safety pins measures 27 inches. Fasten off. Weave in loose end.

December 19: Men's infinity scarf pattern

Materials

Worsted 4 ply yarn

6mm hook

Instructions

Chain 172

Row 1: DC in second ch from hook, DC in rest beginning ch

Row 2: ch 2, turn, DC entire row

Row 3: ch 3, turn, TR entire row

Repeat rows 1-3.

Row 7: ch 2, turn, DC entire row

Row 8: ch 2, turn. DC entire row.

Row 9: OPTIONAL slip stitch top row for "finished look"

December 20: Ripple Tie

Materials

Sport Yarn 1-2 oz red, white, and orange

Crochet hook F

Instruction

Use white, ch 29, sc in 2nd st from hook, 1 sc in each of the next 12 sts of ch, skip 2 chs, 1 sc in the next 13 sts of ch, ch 1, turn.

Row 2: 2 sc in 1st sc, 1 sc in the next 11 sc, skip next 2 sc, 1 sc in next 11 sc, 2 sc in last sc, ch 1, turn.

Repeat row 2 for pattern, working in the following colors: 6 R white, *4 R red, 2 R orange, 4 R red, 4 R orange, 4 R red, 2 R orange, 4 R red, 6 R white. Repeat from * until piece measures 15 inches from beg (measure work at side edge). Discontinue orange and white, work with red for remainder of tie.

NEXT ROW: Work 1 sc in each sc, skip center 2 sc, 1 sc in each sc to end, ch 1, turn.

Repeat last row until there are 12 sc, then continue in pattern as before, working 2 sc in 1st and last sc for 4 ½ inches.

Neck Band: Discontinue to increase in 1st and last st until there are 6 sc, work even on 6 sc until tie measures 48 inches or length desired.

Next row: Decrease 1 sc at beg and end of row, ch 1, turn.

Next row: Work 1 row even.

Next row: Dec 1 st at beg and end of row,

Steam lightly.

December 21: Simple Tie Gift

Materials:

4 ounces 4-ply knitting worsted;

1-ounce mohair for trim

Crochet hook size F

Bow tie clip

Instruction

Tie:

Ch 6. Row 1: Sc in 2nd ch from hook and in each ch across. Ch 1, turn.

Row 2: Sc in each sc across. Ch 1, turn (5 sc).

Repeat this row until tie measures 31½ "

Next row: Work 2 sc in first sc, sc in each sc to last sc, 2 sc in last sc. Ch 1, turn.

Repeat this row 6 times more.

Work even on 19 sc until tie measures 20″ from first inc row. Then dec 1 sc at each edge of every row until 1 sc remains. Fasten off.

Decoration: Attach mohair to wrong side of tie point.

Holding on wrong side, work and crochet hook on right side, draw up a loop, * skip about 1/4″ of work, insert hook and draw up a loop and draw through loop on hook (a sl st), repeat from * keeping tension even.

December 22: Animator's Hat

Materials:

MC: 1 skein Cascade 220

CC: 1 skein Cascade 220

Size J-10 (6.0 mm) crochet hook

Instruction

With MC, ch 2.

Rnd 1. 8 hdc in second ch from hook. Join with sl st to first hdc in rnd. 8 hdc.

Rnd 2. Ch 2; turn. 2 hdc in flo of ea hdc around. Join with sl st to first hdc in rnd. 16 hdc.

Rnd 3. Ch 2; turn. Hdc in flo of first hdc, 2 hdc in flo of next hdc, *1 hdc in flo of next hdc, 2 hdc in flo of next hdc; rep from * around. Join with sl st to first hdc in rnd. 24 hdc.

Rnd 4. Ch 2; turn. Hdc in flo of first 2 hdc, 2 hdc in flo of next hdc, *hdc in flo of next 2 hdc, 2 hdc in flo of next hdc; rep from * around. Join with sl st to first hdc in rnd. 32 hdc.

Rnd 5. Ch 2; turn. Hdc in flo of first 3 hdc, 2 hdc in flo of next hdc, *hdc in flo of next 3 hdc, 2 hdc in flo of next hdc; rep from * around. Join with sl st to first hdc in rnd. 40 hdc.

Rnd 6. Ch 2; turn. Hdc in flo of first 4 hdc, 2 hdc in flo of next hdc, *hdc in flo of next 4 hdc, 2 hdc in flo of next hdc; rep from * around. Join with sl st to first hdc in rnd. 48 hdc..

Rnd 7. Ch 2; turn. Hdc in flo of first 5 hdc, 2 hdc in flo of next hdc, *hdc in flo of next 5 hdc, 2 hdc in flo of next hdc; rep from * around. Join with sl st to first hdc in rnd. 56 hdc.

Rnd 8. Ch 2; turn. Hdc in flo of first 6 hdc, 2 hdc in flo of next hdc, *hdc in flo of next 6 hdc, 2 hdc in flo of next hdc; rep from * around. Join with sl st to first hdc in rnd. 64 hdc.

Rnd 9. Ch 2; turn. Hdc in flo of first 7 hdc, 2 hdc in flo of next hdc, *hdc in flo of next 7 hdc, 2 hdc in flo of next hdc; rep from * around. Join with sl st to first hdc in rnd. 72 hdc.

Rnd 10. Ch 2; turn. Hdc in flo of first 8 hdc, 2 hdc in flo of next hdc, *hdc in flo of next 8 hdc, 2 hdc in flo of next hdc; rep from * around. Join with sl st to first hdc in rnd. 80 hdc.

Rnd 11. Ch 2; turn. Hdc in flo of ea hdc around. Join with sl st to first hdc in rnd.

Rnds 12-18. Rep rnd 11.

Change to CC.

Rnds 19-21. Rep rnd 11.

Change to MC.

Rnds 22-24. Rep rnd 11.

Change to CC.

Rnd 25. Rep rnd 11. Finish off. Weave in all ends.

December 23: The Husband Hat

Material:

2 skeins of Patons Classic Merino Wool

I (5.5mm) hook

Instructions

Row1: Using magic ring, sc 6 stitches into ring (6)

Row2: 2 sc in each st. (12)

Row3: (sc in first sc, 2 sc in next sc) around (18)

Row4: (sc in next two sc, 2 sc in next sc) around (24)

Row5: (sc in next three sc, 2 sc in next sc) around (30)

Row6: (sc in next four sc, 2 sc in next sc) around (36)

Row7: (sc in next five sc, 2 sc in next sc) around (42)

Row8: (sc in next six sc, 2 sc in next sc) around (48)

Row9: (sc in next seven sc, 2 sc in next sc) around (54)

Row10: (sc in next eight sc, 2 sc in next sc) around (60)

Row11: (sc in next nine sc, 2 sc in next sc) around (66)

Row12-26 : hdc in each stitch around (66)

Row 27: With contrasting color, sc in each hdc around, join with a sl. st. to first sc. Fasten off and weave in ends. Fold up to desired length.

December 24: Man's Hat

Materials:

Hook Size H/8-5.00MM

Medium (4) Worsted Weight yarn

Instructions

Ch 3. Sl St to first ch to form circle. Ch 3.

Work 15 Dc in circle (16 Dc.)

Row One: Ch 1. Sc in same st . Two Sc in each st (32 sc.)

Sl St to top of 1st st.

Row Two: Ch 2. Hdc in each st. (32 Hdc..)

Sl St to top of 1st Hdc.

Row Three: Ch 1. Sc in same st. Two Sc in each st. (64 Sc.)

Sl St to top of 1st Sc.

Row Four: Ch 2. One Hdc in each st. (64 Hdc.)

Sl St to top of 1st Hdc.

Row Five: Ch 1. One Sc in each stitch (64 Sc.)

Sl St to top of 1st Sc.

REPEAT Row 4 &5 until hat measures 8 inches

Tie off/weave-hide yarn ends.

December 25: Crocheted Wedding Bow Tie

Materials

1 skein Rowan Classic Silk Wool DK, 109yds (100m) in #305 Clay

Yarn needle

Size F5 (3.75mm) hook

Size D3 (3.25mm) hook

Instruction

Step 1: Crochet bow A.

With size F hook, ch 4.

Row 1 (RS) Sc in 2nd ch from hook and in each

ch across, turn — 3 sc.

Row 2 Ch 1, 2 sc in first sc, sc in next sc, 2 sc in last sc, turn — 5 sc.

Row 3 Ch 1, 2 sc in first sc, sc in each sc across up to last sc, 2 sc in last sc, turn — 7 sc.

Rows 4–5 Ch 1, sc in each sc across, turn — 7 sc.

Rows 6–11 Repeat rows 3–5 twice — 11 sc.

Row 12 Repeat row 3, turn — 13 sc.

Rows 13–22 Ch 1, sc in each sc across, turn — 13 sc.

Row 23 Ch 2, sc2tog over first 2 sc, sc in each sc across up to last 2 sc, sc2tog, turn — 11 sc.

Rows 24–25 Ch 1, sc in each sc across, turn — 11 sc.

Rows 26–31 Repeat rows 23–25 twice — 7 sc.

Rows 32–33 Repeat row 23 — 3 sc.

Row 34 Ch 1, sc in each sc across, turn — 3 sc.

Rows 35–49 Repeat rows 2–17 — 13 sc.

Fasten.

Step 2: Crochet bow B.

Ch 4.

Row 1 (RS) Sc in 4th ch from hook and each ch across, turn — 3 sc.

Row 2 Ch 1, sc in each sc across, turn — 3 sc.

Repeat row 2 until band measures 6″ longer than the circumference of the wearer's neck.

Repeat rows 2–49 of bow A.

Fasten off.

December 26: Grown-Ups Easy 'Booties'

Materials

Size J Hook

2 strands of Simply Soft yarn, 2 oz of each

Instructions

Ch 50

ROW 1: Sc in 2nd ch from hook, sc in each st across, ch 1 and turn

ROW 2 - 12: Sc in each sc across, ch 1, turn.

On the end of Row 12, do not ch 1, just turn.

ROW 13: sl st into 1st (13) (17 sts). Ch 1 (counts as a sc) then sc in the next 23 sts (26 sts) - leaving 13 sts (17) unworked. Ch 2 and turn.

ROW 14-15: Dc in the middle stitches, ch 2 and turn

LAST ROW: Alternate 1 fpdc, then 1 bpdc across.

Finish.

December 27: Fingerless Gloves for Men

Materials:

Medium Weight Yarn

Crochet Hook H (5.00 mm)

Yarn Needle   crochet yarn size 4

Instructions

Row 1: ch 34, dc in third ch form hook, dc in each ch across: 32 dc

Row 2 – 11: ch 2, turn, dc in each dc across: 32 dc

Use yarn needle to sew sides of glove together leaving a 2" (5 cm) hole 1" (2.5 cm) from the end.

December 28: Basketball Hoop

Materials

4 ply yarn - 5 yards orange, 6 yards crochet cotton.

One 8" green chenille stem.

Stuffing.

3/4" magnet.

Crochet hook size G and #4 steel hook.

Instructions

Rnd 1: With G hook and orange, ch2, 5 sc in 2nd ch from hook (5).

Rnd 2: 2 sc in each st around (10).

Rnd 3: Sc in each st around.

Rnd 4: (Sc in next st, 2 sc in next st) around (15).

Rnd 5: Sc in each st around.

Rnd 6: (Sc next 2 sts tog) 7 times, sc in last st (8). Stuff.

Rnd 7: (Sc next 2 sts tog) around (4). Leaving 6" for sewing, fasten off. Sew opening closed.

Hoop

Twist 1/4" on each end of chenille stem tog to from ring.

Rnd 1: With #4 steel hook and using crochet cotton, join with sc around ring, ch 10, (sc around ring, ch10) 6 times, join with sl st in first sc (7loops).

Rnd 2: Sl st in first 6 ch, ch 10, (sc in next ch 10 lp, ch 10) around, join with sl st in first sl st.

Rnd 3: Sl st in first 6 ch, ch 6, (sc in next ch 10 lp, ch 6) around, join as before.

Rnd 4: Sl st in first 4 ch, ch 6, (sc in next ch 6 lp, ch 6) around, join.

Fasten off. Glue magnet to outside of hoop.

December 29: Little Boys' Bobble Scarf

Yarn of choice

Crochet hook N

Instructions

Foundation chain: Ch 11

Row 1-3: sc into each stich, turn

Row 4: sc into next 3 sc, *MB (work 4 open dc into same st leaving 5 loops on hook, draw yarn through all 5 loops at once). 1 sc into each of next 2 sc, rep from * twice. sc into next 3 sc.

Rep rows 1-4 until you have the length that you would like.

December 30: Alpaca Weave Scarf

Materials

Blue Sky Alpacas

One skein Bulky

Crochet hook N (10mm)

Instructions

Ch 102

Row 1: in third ch from hook work 1 dc. work 1 dc in next, *ch 1, skip 1, 1 dc in next, 1 dc in next* repeat until you reach the beg of the chain, end

Weave yarn: take 4 strands of yarn about 8 inches longer than the scarf each end (length of yarn for tassels) and weave in the chain spaces

December 31: Lizzy Scarf Pattern

Materials:

K hook

Worsted weight yarn

Instructions

Row 1:

(Ch 6, 2 dtr in 6th ch from hook, (3 loops on hook); yo, draw thru all 3 loops

ch 1)

Repeat until you reach the length you want your scarf to be, be sure to end with an even number of clusters.

Row 1: hold last loop of each st on hook until told to draw thru

Step 1: ch 6, 2 dtr in 6th ch from hook (3 loops on hook)

Step 2: 3 dtr in first eye (6 loops on hook); yo, draw thru all 6 loops; Ch 1 to close cluster

Step 3: ch 6, 2 dtr in 6th ch from hook (3 loops on hook)

Step 4: 3 dtr in same space as last cluster (6 loops on hook)

Step 5: 3 dtr in next eye (9 loops on hook); yo, draw thru all 9 loops

ch 1 to close cluster

Row 2:

Repeat row 1

Conclusion

With these patterns, anyone who wishes to learn one or two things about crocheting is in a good position to do just that. There is a pattern for every single day of the year. You can make something special and give them to someone as a gift.

Once you go through the entire list for the year, you might perhaps come across some of the patterns that you would consider favorites, and choose to repeat them more often.

There are patterns that you can get extra creative with, and determine the length you want. For some of them you can also play around with the yarn colors and so forth.

One of the most important things that we have to stress on these projects is that once you get the basics, you can feel free to be as creative as you desire. In the long run, it is all about bringing out the crochet wizard in you, and you will enjoy crocheting every other time that you can find time.